# Praise for Ann
## and *Study Smar*

"Calling all teenagers (and their exasp...
putting off calling Procrastinators Ar..............................
that work for you, this is the book for you. If you spend hours 'studying' without seeing your grades improve, this is the book for you. If
you are starting to realize that acting too cool for school isn't cool at
all, this is the book for you. In short, if you are a teenager who wants
to do better in school while gaining a sense of self (and maybe even a
social life) this is the book for you."
   —Ginger Fay, President, Fay College Counseling, LLC

"Anne Crossman demystifies studying, proving that academic success
isn't magic. . . . Her book is accessible and helpful for ALL students,
particularly those transitioning to high school. Parents, teachers,
and counselors who want to help their kids succeed would also do
well to read it."
   —Brian Cooper, Director of Educational Programs,
      Duke University Talent Identification Program

"As a school counselor and former college admissions director, I have
run across many smart students who were not successful because
they didn't know how to study. *Study Smart, Study Less* is custom made
for these kids. What makes this book different is that it helps students
identify their study style and teaches them how to maximize their
strengths. Anne Crossman has given new hope to students who want
to improve their study skills and boost their academic performance."
   —Gordon E. Stanley, PhD, Director of Counseling, Marist School

# STUDY SMART, STUDY LESS

- **Earn Better Grades and Higher Test Scores**
- **Learn Study Habits That Get Fast Results**
- **Discover Your Study Persona**

## ANNE CROSSMAN

### ILLUSTRATIONS BY CHRIS KALB

Ten Speed Press
Berkeley

*Josiah, Isaiah, and Evelyn*
*may you excel in all that your hearts desire*

Copyright © 2011 by Anne Crossman
Illustrations © 2011 by Chris Kalb

All rights reserved.
Published in the United States by Ten Speed Press, an imprint of the
Crown Publishing Group, a division of Random House, Inc., New York.
www.crownpublishing.com
www.tenspeed.com

Ten Speed Press and the Ten Speed Press colophon are registered
trademarks of Random House, Inc.

Library of Congress Cataloging-in-Publication Data
Crossman, Anne, author.
Study smart, study less : earn better grades and higher test scores,
learn study habits that get fast results, and discover your study
persona / Anne Crossman. — First edition.
     p. cm
  Includes index.
 1.  Study skills.  I. Title.
  LB1049.C775 2011
  371.3'0281—dc22

                                        2010046307

ISBN 978-1-60774-000-1

Printed in the United States

Design by Colleen Cain

10 9 8 7 6 5 4 3 2 1

First Edition

# CONTENTS

# PREFACE:
## *Study* Is Not a Four-Letter Word

Chances have it that if you're trying to learn how to improve your study habits it's because you have studying to do, which means **you probably don't have oodles of time to read massive books about how to study . . . which is why we're here.**

Somewhere between junior high and college, teachers expect that you will have magically learned how to study. I have no idea where they get *that* idea since few schools actually offer courses in how to take notes, and, to be fair, most teachers have more material to teach than they do time. As a result, study skills rarely work into the lesson plan, leaving you without the skills you need to reach your academic potential . . . which is why we're here.

There are some who would swear *study* is a four-letter word. Just the threat of it calls up nightmares about maelstroms of papers to write, monuments of charts to fill, and galaxies of numbers to crunch—all due tomorrow. It's enough to make anyone procrastinate or die a premature, stress-related death . . . which is why we're here.

Studying is all about pacing. It's about studying your brains out without losing your mind. Or, to put it differently, it's about studying to your brain's fullest potential using techniques that are actually easy for you, making you smart while keeping you sane. **So, in an effort to make you as *smart* as possible in a way that is as *painless* as possible in as *little time* as possible, I have written this zesty little guide to get you started on what will hopefully become a lifetime of studiousness and success.** Which, in the end, is why we are here.

# Maniacs, Brainiacs, Geeks, and Slackers

**1**

## Identifying your study persona

We all wish studying were something we could do in our sleep, or that plugging a computer chip into our brains would do the trick. I hate to be the one to break it to you, but here it goes—success requires work. I know that's just an awful thing to say, but **becoming a successful student requires a lot of sweat, sacrifice, and diligence. No great shocker there.** However, that doesn't mean work can't be fun. With the right outlook, tools, and expectations, you might be surprised how enjoyable academic success can be.

Very few people are naturally organized or get good grades without trying—and the few who are true natural geniuses in contrast have to work harder at things that seem normal to the rest of us. Everyone has different talents. As we work through this book, I intend to help you discover your learning strengths so that you will not only know how to make the most of them, but will also feel more confident as you tackle areas where you may not be as strong.

Wanting to do well but not knowing how is enough to drive anyone batty. Like the title of this chapter alludes, if we're truly honest with ourselves we will admit that we all have a little bit of slacker in us. I mean, let's be real. . . . Who is genuinely 100 percent thrilled to work? That said, work is one of those unavoidable realities, and when it comes our way it turns some of us into maniacs, some of us into geeks, and a lucky few into pumpkins—I mean, brainiacs. Fortunately for you, you are reading this book and are, therefore, well on your way to the latter.

Before we can begin to maximize your strengths (that's the next chapter), we need to first identify your study persona. The whole reason you're reading this book is because you think you could be doing better in class than you currently are. As a former high school English teacher I can tell you that, when faced with work, students tend to veer toward one of the four following study personas. Understanding which one you resemble most will help you pinpoint your study needs better. So, read on and mark the one that fits you best (we're going for the most similarities here).

**THE UNPERFECTED PERFECTIONIST:** You try really hard, you pull all-nighters, and you get nowhere. How frustrating. **You seem to be doing everything right (and sometimes you have the grades to show you're trying), but the end result isn't meeting your expectations.** Maybe the grade wasn't high enough. Or, you can't seem to remember what you studied so hard to learn earlier in the quarter when it comes time to take the final. Either way, you're wishing you could throw in the towel because your hard work is just not paying off.

**THE DEADLINE DAREDEVIL:** You think you work better under pressure and insist on waiting until the night before the deadline to start your project, hoping all your lucky stars will align and the printer won't go on strike. It seems like a good plan. After all, when have adrenaline and sheer terror not been good motivators? Still, you find yourself having to repeat the cram session all over again when it comes time for the midterm, and then again for the final. And, when you tried to impress that good-looking someone last week with your knowledge of the Han Dynasty, you drew a blank. For the short term your plan seems to be working. But **some days it feels like all you're doing is putting out one deadline fire after another, which is causing you to sprout gray hairs prematurely.**

**THE MACK SLACKER:** You have perfected your art of doing nothing and doing it well. When it comes time to see the scores, you are the only one who really knows what you're getting and you put on a fairly convincing show that you don't really care. Classmates seem to love you for the fact that you don't study, don't pass, and don't care. But—though you wouldn't admit it to them—**you are starting to wonder how to get from "chill" to "millionaire," and you aren't sure if your Aunt Tilda bought enough lottery tickets for your plan to pay off.**

**THE BRAIN TRAINER:** You have a balanced amount of time and play that allow you to learn the material, pass the test, and actually have a life. You have a variety of effective study habits and techniques at your fingertips that make your time behind the desk efficient and, most important, memorable. **When a deadline or exam comes, you are pretty relaxed because you know that you know the material.** If this is you, maybe *you* should write a book! Seriously, though, even if this *is* you, *keep reading*—I have more tools to add to your arsenal.

# Getting Your Money's Worth

Now that you've identified your study persona, I'd like to suggest some specific sections to focus on as you read through the remaining chapters. You'll still want to read the whole book (and in order, preferably) to make sure you're getting your money's worth out of the deal. After you've finished reading everything from how to make your brain work for you to what Whoopi Goldberg and Albert Einstein have in common, come back to this chapter and read over these suggestions once more to see if anything pops.

The **Unperfected Perfectionist** is someone who clearly has a good work ethic but feels a bit lost about how to make sure all that hard work pays off. If this is you, you'll want to identify your learning strengths in chapter two and pay close attention to the study tricks in chapter four, as well as various note-taking tips in chapter five. For you, the drive to do well is already there—which for most people is the hardest part. So, take heart.

Once you work through the book and figure out your learning strengths and specific study strategies, you'll be better equipped to beat the books and make the grade in no time. On the off chance all this isn't enough and your grades are still dropping, don't panic. Before you get completely frustrated and turn into a Mack Slacker, read through chapter six. You may have some hidden land mines that are hurting your chances for success, simply because you haven't yet learned how to tiptoe around them.

The **Deadline Daredevil** is someone who needs a monstrous kick in the rear to get work done. If this is you, you might consider tracking down your favorite role model (preferably NOT a parent or peer for this scheme) and ask that person to check up on you (meaning, he should ask you specific questions about how your studying is going).

Call it Procrastinators Anonymous, if you like. The point is that you need someone who can look at your assignment calendar with you and help you learn how to restructure your life so you *get work done early*. (Of course, this requires having an assignment calendar in the first place—look for insider advice on that in chapter three.)

Part of what makes learning so *unmemorable* for you is that you're studying under stress. Understanding how your brain works (see chapter two) will be critical in motivating you to work ahead of your deadlines. And, creating a dependable study environment (see chapter three) will show you how to use your time more effectively. It's critical that you feel comfortable with these two chapters (as far as understanding what needs to be done and being willing to do it . . . not necessarily liking it just yet) before you move on to the rest.

The **Mack Slacker** is someone who has convinced others (and perhaps even himself) that he believes grades don't matter. But he doesn't know how to meet his goals and so is at least willing to flip through the first few pages of this book. If that is you, thank you. Seriously. For whatever reason, studying is not your thing, but you have given this book a chance and I appreciate it.

To be honest, this book will make a lot more sense once you figure out what has made studying so awful for you. Is it a fear of failure (and you don't bother trying so you won't feel bad)? Is it that you don't know where to start (and you feel awkward asking for help), so you have given up? If you answered yes to either of these, check out chapter five, which addresses the most common complaints students have about studying. (You can even skip ahead to it first and then read the rest of the book later, though there might be a few points that won't completely make sense until you read the preceding chapters.)

However, if you don't know what has made studying seem so irrelevant, read through the book and pay close attention to chapter six. You might even make an appointment with a school counselor. Believe it or not, school counselors are absolutely hoping you will do just that . . . really. You'll make their day. They may even give you a pass to meet with them during class. If you don't feel comfortable doing that, meet with a teacher during lunch and *take this book with you* so you can work through it together. Your teacher might have some insights into what is causing your struggles and how to best apply key points in this book to your situation. The bottom line is that someone ate your breadcrumb trail and now you need a bit of help finding your way out of the woods.

The **Brain Trainer** is someone who has mastered the art of studying and feels confident that success is on the way. If this is you, you'll want to keep reading. Yes, I know I said earlier that you should write your own book, but this one is already here for you so why not make use of it? I've known Ivy League graduates (meaning Harvard, Duke, and Stanford types) who have read this book and learned something new about themselves in the process. So, don't sell yourself short. It's a quick read, and it's very likely you'll learn something.

THE BRAIN TRAINER

# Unlocking Your Inner Brainiac

**2**

## Identifying and maximizing your learning strengths

Learning something new is all about getting your brain to do its job the way *it wants to* do its job. Don't underestimate that three-pound hunk of gray matter—it truly has a mind of its own. So, stay focused as you read this chapter. Yes it's about the brain, but I promise it's not as hard as brain surgery.

## The Long and Short of It

To use any machine properly, it helps to know a little about it, which is why this chapter is worth your time. The brain is the most complex computer unknown to man, and scientists are constantly finding themselves baffled and amazed by this little organ. Weighing only three pounds, the brain controls all communications with your other body parts, as well as how your body communicates with other bodies. Basically, **the brain affects absolutely everything about your life, which is kind of scary considering how relatively little we know about it.** For the sake of time, we'll save the lecture on The Amazing Brain for your psychology class and stick to understanding a little more about memory.

There are three basic categories for memory: **Short-Term Memory, Working Memory,** and **Long-Term Memory.** Short-Term Memory remembers seven bits of information (give or take a couple) for a few seconds. It's the sort of memory you use when someone tells you their phone number and you remember it just long enough to get out a piece of paper and write it down. Working Memory is a more active version of Short-Term Memory, and because it is actively manipulating or thinking about the information, the brain is able to retain it a little longer. However, scientists are still debating how long Working Memory can retain information and how clearly it is distinguished from Long-Term Memory and yadda yadda (fill in the blank with heady psychology stuff). So, for the sake of simplicity, we'll just group the two together under the heading "Short-Term Memory," which serves our purposes here just fine, thank you very much. Long-Term Memory is what you'll learn how to activate by reading this book. Essentially, Long-Term Memory stores information for as little as a few days up to decades. To get something into your Short-Term Memory, you need both **Input** and **Output.** For those of you Visual learners who need to see it to get it, here's a formula:

$$\text{Input} + \text{Output} = \text{Short-Term Memory}$$

Input is quite simply putting something into your brain. Whether that is listening to a lecture, reading a book, or reviewing notes, **Input is something *outside* of your head being put *into* your head.** Output is even more exciting because you have so many creative choices at your disposal and it's up to you to decide how to apply what you've learned. Output is important to the memory process because it **takes what you put into your memory and does something with it,** which tells your brain "pay attention, this is important stuff I'll need later."

This is not as complicated as it may sound. We look at thousands of pieces of information every day, making it, at times, difficult for our brains to know which information to keep and which to toss. Fortunately, that's not for your brain to decide—otherwise you'd remember the license plate of a car you passed on the way to school this morning instead of the Civil War notes your teacher wrote on the board this afternoon. Not a plan for success. We have to give our brains cues to make it work for *us*.

**We make a memory *only* when we use (or respond strongly to) information.** By thinking about new information and then doing something active with it, you are essentially telling your brain that this new information is worth remembering. That "doing something" could be drawing charts, making a video, quizzing a friend, or a whole host of other creative possibilities that we'll get to in chapter four. The bottom line is **the more senses you involve in the learning process, the better your chances that you'll remember what you studied.**

All this is great for Short-Term Memory, but what if you want to impress someone under a starry sky by reciting the poems of Robert Frost? How do you get that into your Long-Term Memory (and is it painful)? Whether or not it's painful depends on your point of view, but the good news is that it's easy. It's just review.

> **Input + Output + Review = Long-Term Memory**

It only takes a few hours right before an exam to cram a lot of useless facts into your brain. (Let's face it—if the facts were useful, would you be cramming? And, yes, I will teach you a few tips for successful cramming later on.) But, *it doesn't take much more effort* to start studying earlier so you can review what you studied and actually (*gasp*!) learn something. You've heard the adage "practice makes perfect," but do you know why that holds true?

Imagine a grassy lawn that is between someone's driveway and front door. Rather than walk the long way down the path, around the sidewalk, and up the driveway, most people just cut through the grass to get to their car, right? The more times someone cuts through the grass, the flatter the grass becomes on that new pathway until, eventually, the grass dies back and there is a permanent dirt path. Of course, if no one walks on that path for six months the grass will grow back and begin to fill in the space again. That is pretty much how the brain works. Every time you review something, neurons fire repeat impulses in your brain making that pathway more permanent. Maybe we should really be saying "practice makes memory."

> Information travels between neurons—at its slowest—at a mere 260 mph, faster than the fastest race car: the Bugatti EB 16.4 Veyron, which clocked at 253 mph. At least if you think fast you won't get a speeding ticket.

What that means practically is that if, for the next couple weeks after your test, you review those poems by Robert Frost every few days and then review once a week for a few months thereafter, you'll be on your way to genius—or at least Long-Term Memory. Of course, if after reviewing for those few months you never think of Robert Frost again, your ability to recall the poems will be a bit . . . grassy. **The less you use a piece of information, the further back in your memory your brain will stuff it, and it may take quite a bit of effort to pull it out again.**

Of course, there are some memorization tricks that discount the need to review as often. I mean, why else would you remember the lyrics to *Mary Had a Little Lamb* (a poem I assume you aren't still reading nightly) but you probably can't remember your locker combination from last year? It's not like you are reviewing nursery rhymes on a regular basis, right? Later on in chapter four I'll let you in on a few trade secrets that make memorizing easier. For now, make note that in order to memorize well you need to review, review, review.

## What's Your Strength, Baby?

Incessant note-taking is not quite what our minds had in mind when they signed on for this job. **Everyone's brain works differently, and each person has one or two learning strengths that trigger a whole mental warehouse of storage space. Your brain is desperately hoping you will discover yours so that learning will become a lot more fun and a lot less work.**

The first step to making learning easier, then, is understanding what kind of learner you are. Before I launch into the different learning types, *first* take a moment to answer the following ten questions. Trust me, it's really important that you answer the questions *before* reading the rest of the chapter, and they're a no-brainer. I promise. Just circle the choice that seems the *best* possible answer for you, even though it may not be 100 percent all-the-time true for you. We're aiming for the answer that shows how you would react *most of the time*, and if your perfect answer isn't even listed, my apologies. . . . Just circle whatever is the next most likely answer.

The amount of energy the brain uses is enough to power a 25-watt lightbulb. See, you *are* bright!

1. You remember your new locker combination best when
   a. you say it to yourself over and over again.
   b. you stare at the paper it's printed on and read it over and over again.
   c. you practice unlocking your locker over and over again.

2. If you were trapped in a waiting room for half an hour, you would probably
   a. read a magazine.
   b. pace the room, drum on your knee with your fingers, or be active in some way.
   c. listen to background Muzak piped into the waiting room and let your mind wander.

3. If you were trying to remember where you left your house key, you'd most likely
   a. talk yourself through where you would have had it last.
   b. visualize yourself using the key to open the door and then where you set it next.
   c. walk through the house and retrace your steps.

4. To boost your confidence to ask that special someone to prom you might
   a. go exercise to burn off your jitters and build up courage.
   b. practice what you'd say aloud a few times to get comfortable with the words.
   c. write out a list of all the reasons your special someone should say Yes, and what points you might need to make in order to prevent a *No*.

5. At the end of the term, you tend to remember most easily the work that you
   a. copied into your notes by listening to the lecture.
   b. read from the textbook.
   c. developed into a model.

6. If you wanted to learn how to make a perfect Dairy Queen soft-serve ice cream cone (it's harder than it looks!), you would probably first want to
   a. watch someone else make a soft-serve ice cream cone.
   b. try to make a soft-serve ice cream cone.
   c. listen to someone explain how to make a soft-serve ice cream cone.

7. If you saw a hit-and-run accident and tried to remember the license plate, your first instinct might be to
   a. talk yourself, and possibly someone else, through each step of what you saw until your memory becomes clearer.
   b. close your eyes and reenact what you saw in your mind.
   c. close your eyes and reenact what you felt at the time.

8. If you heard a new song you liked and wanted to learn the lyrics, you'd most likely
   a. read them as you listen to the song.
   b. sing them with the song while it plays, even if you bungle the words badly.
   c. just listen to the song on repeat and try to memorize the lyrics as you hear them.

9. When your mom gives you instructions on how to take out the trash, you're more likely to follow through with what she says if you
   a. do it immediately.
   b. look at the floor and just focus on what she's saying.
   c. look at her face while she talks.

10. If you could design the perfect study environment, it would most likely be
    a. a comfortable temperature that enables you to stretch and move around.
    b. somewhere that has meaningless but steady background noise.
    c. absolutely silent and well lit.

# How'd You Do?

The hardest part of this test, honestly, is adding up the totals correctly. Don't just sum the a's, b's, and c's. First, divide them like you see below and put the proper number of checks into each box.

| Questions | a = Auditory | b = Visual | c = Kinesthetic |
|-----------|--------------|------------|-----------------|
| **1, 3, 5, 7:** 1. | ☐ | ☐ | ☐ |
| 3. | ☐ | ☐ | ☐ |
| 5. | ☐ | ☐ | ☐ |
| 7. | ☐ | ☐ | ☐ |

| Questions | a = Visual | b = Kinesthetic | c = Auditory |
|-----------|------------|-----------------|--------------|
| **2, 6, 8:** 2. | ☐ | ☐ | ☐ |
| 6. | ☐ | ☐ | ☐ |
| 8. | ☐ | ☐ | ☐ |

| Questions | a = Kinesthetic | b = Auditory | c = Visual |
|-----------|-----------------|--------------|------------|
| **4, 9, 10:** 4. | ☐ | ☐ | ☐ |
| 9. | ☐ | ☐ | ☐ |
| 10. | ☐ | ☐ | ☐ |

Totals: _____ Auditory _____ Visual _____ Kinesthetic

    If you don't fit neatly into one category, don't sweat it. **Most people are a combination of two learning strengths.** Your top score will show a *tendency* in your learning style, and if your top two scores are close in number it means you have two strengths to work with when learning something new. Lucky you. Even if you are evenly spread across all three groups, your school counselor will have a more in-depth test you can take to narrow things down.

# Characteristics of Learning Strengths

Learning strengths, also called learning modes or learning styles, tend to be divided into three primary types: Visual, Auditory, and Kinesthetic. (There are even more complex ways to categorize learning strengths using other methods, but for now we're sticking with the basics.)

Your score above will land you in one or two of the following categories, the descriptions of which should sound familiar. However, even if you scored highest in Kinesthetic, it doesn't mean that the entire Kinesthetic description will apply.

So, then, what's the point? The point is to locate where you have your greatest strengths so that when it comes time to learn something new you can work *with* those strengths instead of *against* them. It's part of that *study smarter, not harder* idea. **The easier it is for your brain to learn the material, the quicker you can get your studying finished and the stronger your grades will be.** When we get to study tips in chapter four, I'll make suggestions according to your learning strengths.

**AUDITORY** learners tend to do well in a traditional classroom setting because they naturally understand most of the instructions or information they *hear* from the teacher. (That doesn't necessarily mean Auditory learners will remember that new information, just that it's easier to understand it if someone explains it to them.) If you're an Auditory learner, you may remember people's names just from hearing them the first time or two, you might remember something better if you've said it back aloud to yourself a couple times, perhaps you hum or talk while you work, or you might be able to work well despite noise in the background if it is the type of noise you like.

**VISUAL** learners also tend to do well in a traditional classroom setting because they just need to see it to get it. They learn best with diagrams, charts, pictures, and written directions. If you're a Visual learner, you may like having your To Do list written down, you might be concerned that your notes appear neat on the page, you might remember people's names better if you've seen them written on a name tag or paper at some point, and you may even be great at scheduling things in advance. Perhaps you close your eyes when you need to remember something in order to visualize it first, or you need a quiet place when it comes time to study to help you concentrate.

**KINESTHETIC** learners, unlike the other two, tend to dislike the traditional classroom setting. In fact, the idea of desks in a row and taking notes just about makes them gag. What these students need is hands-on learning, such as performing science experiments, building models, acting in plays, or creating something with glue and toothpicks. If you're a Kinesthetic learner you might understand directions better if you visualize yourself performing them instead of just reading them. Whether or not you mean to, you might tap, draw, or tinker when you're bored, or use gestures when you speak, or remember conversations based on how and where someone was standing at the time.

Whatever your score, it might interest you to know that about 20 to 30 percent of students are Auditory, 40 percent are Visual, and 20 to 30 percent are Kinesthetic. There are no oddballs when it comes to learning strengths, though traditional schools may make Kinesthetic learners feel that way. In fact, researchers believe that some people who have been diagnosed with attention-deficit hyperactivity disorder have been *incorrectly labeled*. It turns out that they are simply Kinesthetic learners whose needs aren't being met in a traditional setting, making them frustrated. Having said that, let me be perfectly clear: the Kinesthetic learning style is NOT a learning disability—it's a skill.

## Making Memorizing Easier

The second step to making learning easier (and opening up that whole mental warehouse of storage space we talked about earlier) is knowing a few things about how your brain stores information. There have been enough reams printed on the subject to fell a whole rain forest, so I'll be brief (otherwise the Kinesthetic folks might start drawing frowny faces in the margins).

> **Brains like patterns!**

Simple enough. **Our brains learn best when what we're trying to learn is arranged into groups.** (Hence this book has been organized into chapters and sections.) Whether we realize it or not, we are constantly organizing our life into groups: finishing the easy homework first . . . remembering (or, more likely, saving on speed dial) telephone numbers of people according to how much we like to talk with them . . . categorizing our mothers' friends as those with hairstyles trapped in the last century and those we wouldn't mind being seen with in public . . . you get the idea.

In other words, the fastest way to help your brain learn something is to help it see patterns by first organizing the information into groups. So, if you're memorizing verbs for your Italian class, first separate them into regular and irregular verbs. Then, within those two categories, group them according to the type of job they describe or by what they have in common. This means putting all of the regular verbs that have to do with noise in one group (such as to sing, to speak, to scream, to honk) and all the regular verbs that have to do with, oh, let's say an adrenaline rush in another group (such as to jump, to skydive, to scuba). Heck, you can even doodle next to each verb if you're a Visual or Kinesthetic learner to help you remember. Regardless of the doodles, seeing those actions grouped together will help you remember which verbs are regular and which are irregular and therefore how to conjugate them to suit your needs, and that will come in handy when you meet the stylish foreign exchange student at school and want to conjugate *to go to the movies* on the quick.

The same holds true for memorizing math functions. Just ask yourself what the functions do, group them accordingly, and, most importantly, study them in those groups. What about English vocabulary? Historical themes? Chemical compounds? Yes, they can all be organized into some sort of group or pattern.

As well as organizational patterns, **our brains learn especially well when there is some sort of emotion involved.** So, feel free to organize your chemical compounds into groups of *things that smell disgusting* or *things I'd like to light on fire* or *things I'm worried may blow up in my face*—your brain is sure to remember. **It may require some creativity on your part to find patterns in what you're learning, but that sort of active studying is exactly the kind of Output your brain needs in order to recognize that this is information you want to keep.**

# ON THE CATWALK

At the end of every chapter, I'll model good review practices by summarizing what you just learned. This is a bonus for you on two fronts. First, you get to see a few different examples of what summary notes might look like so you can do it with your class work at school. Second, I do your work for you so you can remember the key points from this book. (You can thank me later.)

1. **The long and short of it** is that our brains have both Long- and Short-Term Memories—the longer we review it the longer it's stored.
   - Input + Output = Short-Term Memory
   - Input + Output + Review = Long-Term Memory
   - Input = into our brains, Output = use it
2. **What's your strength, baby?**
   - Visual learners need to see it to learn it.
   - Auditory learners need to hear or say it to learn it.
   - Kinesthetic learners need to be active with it to learn it.
3. **Characteristics of learning strengths**
   - I took the test and I am a _____ learner.
4. **Making memorizing easier**
   - Brains like patterns (such as putting verbs about making noise in one group and verbs about quiet activities in another when I'm studying French).
   - Be creative. The extra thinking required to make these groups of patterns is actually great Output that will help me learn.

THE UNPERFECTED PERFECTIONIST

# Rescuing the Book-Laden, Burned-Out, and Bewildered Student    **3**

## Small changes to your work style that lead to big results

So, you've read about the brain, you know what your study persona is, you know your primary learning strength, and you're ready to get down to work. Even more important than study tricks and learning strengths, however, is your study environment. **If the setup isn't right, you're going to waste a lot of time and learn very little** (even if you use the amazing study tricks you'll learn about in the next chapter). Fortunately, it only takes a few changes to your study setup to help your brain work *for* you so that you study more efficiently and, therefore, spend less time studying.

## Give Yourself Some Space

The hardest part of studying for most people is actually the first part: sitting down. Granted, there are at least eight other things you'd rather be doing right now, like having your teeth cleaned. The best thing you can do for yourself, then, is to work to your strengths so that you can get the studying over with and make a date with your favorite hygienist. Here are a couple of suggestions to get you and your surroundings ready to study smarter and study less.

**DECIDE ON A TIME AND PLACE** where you can study every day after school. Since the good TV shows tend to come on later in the evening, it's wise to get your work done before then. Or, better yet, record the shows so you can watch them when your work is done (and save time by skipping through commercials). **The absolute best place to study is at a table or desk. Don't EVEN try to read in bed—your brain has been programmed that the bed is where you sleep, and trying to convince it otherwise is futile.** The couch is another no-no for the same reason. Train your brain to know the difference between work time and play time by studying in places that make your brain snap to attention *Oh! . . . this talented body of mine wants me to learn something.* Also, make sure your desk has good lighting to prevent eyestrain and headaches.

**KEEP NECESSARY MATERIALS AT YOUR STUDY SPOT** (such as extra pencil lead, a dictionary, water, and pistachios) so they are waiting for you when you need them. If planning ahead is not your forte, do a quick inventory and write a neon sticky note at the end of your study session if it looks like you're running low on something. In my formerly ill-prepared days, I spent seemingly half my time running things up and down the stairs because they weren't in the place I needed them when it was time to get my work done; it was great exercise but not great efficiency. Believe me, this is a smarter way to go.

**ELIMINATE AS MANY DISTRACTIONS AS POSSIBLE** by turning off your cell phone and steering clear of chats when you're trying to study; otherwise, every time Betty pings you you'll lose your place in *The Odyssey* and have to go back and reread the section. The same goes for avoiding email, YouTube, surfing, and all online "in-your-friends'-business-every-second" sites. You know the ones I mean. **Give yourself the freedom and space to socially check out for a couple hours so you can get some work done. Your friends will understand, and if they don't . . . well . . . maybe they aren't such great friends.** On the other hand, who knows. Maybe your study hour will inspire your friends to do the same. Stranger things have happened.

If your work requires you to use a computer, as is often the case, refrain from opening your favorite browser tabs or logging into your social networks until your work is done, so that they don't sit on-screen flashing their ads and invitations to chat, tempting you to take "just a five-second break." During my stint as an editor, I once had a slow day at work, so I logged onto a chat room; two hours of random conversations with strangers later, I was shocked to see the time stamp, especially since I had hardly gotten a thing done. Sheesh, those are two hours of my life I'll never get back.

As much as it may pain you, turn off the television and all music. Your brain will be able to work much faster if it's not (subconsciously) concentrating so hard to block out the noise or images. My students would frequently insist that listening to music while they studied actually helped them study, so I'll let you in on the same secret I told them: **you may *think* listening to music helps you study more efficiently, but what it actually does is help pass the time,** making it seem like you've studied quickly when you've actually been sitting there longer than you should have because you're being lulled by the tunes. My students would typically acknowledge that point but persist, saying that listening to music helped them survive the evening. That may be. However, I ask you—as I did them—this question: would you rather spend four hours studying poorly *with music* or two and a half hours *in silence* with the remaining hour and a half to use however you like? Those numbers are just an estimate, but you get the idea. Hopefully you'll opt for efficiency and shut off the tunes.

**DRESS FOR THE OCCASION,** which may require your disbelief for a moment. Scientists have actually discovered an honest-to-goodness Mr. Rogers Syndrome showing that people who wear clothes that relate to their goals perform better. Remember when Mr. Rogers came home for the afternoon and changed from his work coat into his comfy sweater to tell us stories? That was a signal that playtime had started, and he always changed back into the coat when he headed back to work. Give it a try. I found it startling how much it improved my ability to focus when I donned my study uniform. (Nope, I'm not going to tell you what it was . . . that one I'll keep to myself.)

> When you were just a "bun in the oven" in the first few months of life, your brain grew at the rate of 250,000 neurons a minute. Way to go, baby.

A great example of how this can have the opposite affect is Pajama Day at school. Think back on how hard it was to focus when you were sitting at your desk in flannels or how goofy your classmates may have been behaving. I'll be honest, as a teacher it was one of my least favorite days during Spirit Week because my students carried on as though class was one big slumber party. It was nearly impossible to get anything done.

Please understand, I'm not recommending you go out and buy a wool cardigan for your study hour; just that you change out of your Doctor Dentons into something that signals you're about to get down to business. **Think of study clothes as one of those flashing construction signs on the side of the road that signals "Work in Progress."** While you'll want to wear something comfortable, pajamas or sweats are a bad idea. . . . They communicate sleep and lounging, which is not what you're about to do. At the same time, your study uniform doesn't need to look like something straight off a prep school campus; it's up to you to discern the prop or attire that works best for you.

I had one student, Becca, who reluctantly agreed to test out this concept by wearing an inexpensive pair of wire glasses with no prescription in the lenses because she thought they might make her feel smart, studious, and potentially more focused. She only wore the specs when she studied at home, but even with that she told me after a few weeks that her grades had jumped from C to B and B to A simply by incorporating the glasses and a few other setup strategies into her homework routine. Weird, I know. But it works.

If dressing up isn't your gig, a study ritual is also a possibility. Mr. Rogers sang "Won't You Be My Neighbor" at the beginning of every episode. You could incorporate your own brain-stimulating theme song, such as listening to classical music *right before* (as opposed to during) your study session to get your head in the game. Aaron Copland was a favorite in my classroom, if you're looking for suggestions.

Remember, **our brains love patterns and structure, so providing a routine for studying will help your focus and productivity more than you may initially give it credit.** As a parallel example, many professional athletes profess to have their own unique pre-game rituals that they swear by to help them get on their game faces before leaving the locker room, saying they can't be 110 percent without them. Whatever your opponent, hopefully you've found a study space that is quiet and maybe even private so that if you decide to wear a lab coat because it makes writing chemistry reports easier, you won't feel like a big geek.

> About three full soda cans worth of blood flow through the brain every minute. Talk about going right to your head.

**PUT YOUR GOALS WHERE YOU CAN SEE THEM** to help them seem more achievable. Maybe seeing our goals all the time helps our minds stay focused on achieving them. Maybe it helps our will keep wanting them. Whatever the reason, it works.

Let me emphasize that **goals need to be both specific and realistic.** An example of a bad goal would be "get good grades" not because it isn't a good thing to want but because it's hard to measure improvement. "Get an A in Chemistry this quarter" is a much better goal because it is clear—how realistic that may be is for you to decide. A friend of mine once taped pieces of paper all over her room with A's on them to remind her to keep her expectations high; another taped Monopoly money by his desk, since his goal was to make grades that could lead to an immediate boost in his allowance, as well as future entrance to a great college and a strong degree. Neither was a specific goal, but both were certainly motivational, which is better than nothing. Obviously, "winning the lottery" flunks on both accounts.

The idea is to remind yourself why you're working so hard so that your goals seem achievable. Be sure to set long-term goals (such as the Monopoly money representing the college degree) and short-term goals (like "Get an A on my research paper," or "Finish the novel by Friday") that get you closer to your long-term goals so you have something in the distant future to aim for as well as more frequent reasons to celebrate. **Celebrating every short-term goal you reach builds a sense of satisfaction that will help you stay motivated and keep working toward your long-term goals.**

So, take a moment to set a few specific, realistic short- and long-term goals, and then hang them up where you will bump into them frequently or when you may need them most—inside your locker door, beside your bed, or at the sink where you brush your teeth.

# It's All About Timing

The key to your success is taking control of your schedule so that you are choosing when and how to complete assignments in a way that maximizes your time, instead of surviving with that terrible feeling of always being behind. Planning ahead is much easier than it may sound.

**YOU WIN A PRIZE! After completing one of your short-term goals, you should absolutely reward yourself.** Depending on your budget and taste buds, that reward could be anything—a DQ Peanut Buster Parfait (my personal favorite), a night out at the movies, a neck massage, a new color of nail polish, a new basketball net, that mechanical pencil you've been dreaming about, a full day off from studying, or a sticky star taped to your bulletin board. (I awarded myself one for tenacity when I was in a particularly tough spot a few years ago and it's still hanging on my bulletin board to encourage me over the next speed bump.) Do what will encourage you most.

Keep your prizes small so that you can award them to yourself as needed without breaking the bank. If you have a stressful week full of deadlines or exams, you might need a couple extra rewards in there to keep you going. At the same time, other weeks might not need any at all. As long as you don't go broke by throwing a party every time you finish a page in your calculus textbook (moderation is key here), you may find this to be one of your favorite study strategies.

**TAKE A BREAK.** No, you didn't just misread that heading. (Wahoo! Prizes and study breaks? This is the best study guide ever!) **The best thing to do when you have a big evening of studying ahead of you is not to try and finish everything in one sitting; you will either go crazy and be locked in a rubber room on test day or zone out**

**and remember nothing.** Instead, every twenty to thirty minutes (or when you feel really antsy) get up from your desk and do something totally unrelated to class work for about five minutes. If you've been working on the computer, you'll want your break to be something totally non-techie, the big reason being that it helps prevent eyestrain. (Just ask your ophthalmologist.) Don't do like I did with my chat room at work, expecting your brain will automatically keep track of the time (oops)— be sure you set a timer or you might end up taking a twenty-minute break instead (nuts). Great five-minute breaks might be as follows:

- Give yourself a pedicure with that new polish you earned and paint your nails.
- Take a quick shower.
- Wrestle with your dog.
- Help your mom do the dishes and ask her about her day (really!).
- Play a video game (only five minutes . . . get a timer!).
- Do fifty sit-ups/push-ups.
- Take three ultra-deep breaths and then yawn as many times as you can in sixty seconds (find out why in chapter five).
- Turn on your favorite song and sing loudly.
- Have a snack (hint: protein and veggies are better for brain cells than sugar and soda, the latter causing your blood sugar levels to tank thirty minutes later).
- Walk to the kitchen and get yourself a glass of water— I just did. Don't I sound more alert?

A group of students from my freshman English class really loved the pedicure study break idea, and every time I passed back an exam where they had scored well they would proudly wiggle their newly painted toes and giggle "it worked!" Incidentally, Becca (fake-glasses-girl from earlier) was part of the pedi-painted pack.

**PACE YOURSELF.** Fundamental to all these environmental face-lifts is the assumption that during your study time you will actually know what to study. If *I didn't know that was due today* is your worst nightmare—or daily reality—meet your salvation. **Of all the study setups we've discussed, there is one that is absolutely not optional: the assignment calendar.**

It's true that challenging your brain to remember important details without writing them down is a super exercise to keep your mind sharp. Folks nearing retirement age are encouraged to maintain mental lists, as well as work on sudoku puzzles and all other sorts of brain games, to ward off Alzheimer's and dementia. Even though I'm nowhere near the age of owning my own pink stucco villa, I like to write a grocery list and then leave at home when I go to the market as a way of testing my memory. Okay, maybe I just forgot the list, but rather than kicking myself down the dairy aisle it makes it feel like more of a game.

All that said, with something as critical as a due date, playing mind games is not a wise plan.

**Trying to remember unwritten details is great for security codes, locker combinations, and website passwords—but not homework assignments.** So, head off to an office supply store and pick up a spiral *calendar* notebook. My favorite kind is the 8 x 10-inch type where, when you open it up, you see the full month of September at once, with each day being at least an inch squared. (You will want the squares to be at least that size so you can fit everything in.) I use the term *calendar* as opposed to *assignment book* for a specific reason. First off, you'll want something thin. Assignment books are getting bulkier all the time, with special sections for phone numbers, addresses, time zones, and a bunch of other useless pages. Try to avoid the paper trap. You already have enough books in your bag to send your chiropractor to Fiji, so let's lighten the load and keep this book thin. Because a calendar has only twelve months, and an assignment book is often organized by weeks, you're looking at twelve pages as opposed to fifty-two—a big difference.

The second reason I recommend a month-per-page calendar versus a weekly assignment book is because, for some reason, teachers have an odd penchant for scheduling tests and essays due Monday. (I include myself in this category, much to my shame.) If your assignment book only shows one week at a time, you will think your weekend is free and clear and find yourself sitting in class Monday morning, flipping the page over to a new week and—*GASP*!—staring at those awful words: Due Today. Talk about nightmares. There is also the added benefit that **if you have one month on a page and can see the whole thing at once, it will be easier to manage your time strategically by working ahead.** A quick glance at the calendar will show you that you have a soccer tournament in three weekends *and* a paper due the Monday after. However, because you are seeing it now—three whole weeks in advance—you have time to get the paper done a week early so you can spend the rest of the time polishing your cleats. And gloating.

It's estimated that the human brain racks up 70,000 thoughts in an average day. I wonder if that number doubles during homecoming week.

Of course, a calendar is only helpful if it's within easy reach. The trick is to keep it in your bag at all times so you know where to find it—especially toward the end of class when teachers tend to shout out upcoming deadlines as the bell rings. That way you have a place (other than your hand) to jot down those critical dates. Some teachers like to sprinkle deadlines in with their notes as they lecture, so it might be extra smart to pull your calendar out with your notebook *at the beginning of class.* This is another bonus of your month-at-once booklet being thin—it can lie under your notebook quite comfortably and fit into your front backpack pocket easily without sacrificing space or making your hand wobble on your desk while you take notes.

**Writing down the assignment is only the first half of the solution; be sure you understand what it means *before* you leave the classroom.** Getting a passing grade is near impossible when you're confused. Most teachers will be happy to provide an excuse to your next class if the explanation makes you late, assuming you were attentive during class. If yours isn't willing or gives you grief about it, just show him this chapter where I suggest he provide an excuse and hopefully he'll go along with it—peer pressure works at all ages. Of course, if you slept through class or weren't paying attention the first time around, I'm going to be of little help to you.

## Be Realistic and Stay Positive

Less is sometimes more when it comes to keeping your focus. **If you sit down to a biology chapter with the intention that it will take you all night to read it, then it will take you all night to read it. But, if you tell your brain "I'm going to read as much of this chapter as possible in the next twenty minutes and then go walk the dog," you'll be amazed at how focused you are,** and at how many more pages you're able to get through. The dog will also be impressed when you tell him what you learned about cell division while you stroll around the block.

# Catch Some Zzzzs

A good night's sleep (meaning at least seven uninterrupted hours) is critical to setting yourself up for success. **Pulling all-nighters or working past midnight may make you sound like Student of the Year, but it will actually cripple your attempts to do well on tomorrow's test.** Scientists discovered this when they tracked the brain impulses of rats as they learned their way around a maze, and then tracked the brain impulses of these same rats as they slept. It turns out that once the rats slipped into a deep sleep, their brains actually re-sent many of the same impulses they had sent while learning the maze earlier in the day—their brains were reviewing while snoozing! Fortunately for humans, our brains use sleep in a similar way—talk about getting your cheese and eating it too. The point is, don't let your study time interfere with your bedtime. Sleeping off what you just learned is practically as important as the time you spent learning it, which is a fabulous incentive to hit the sack. Of course, there's nothing more insomnia inspiring than a looming deadline. If you're the type of person who has consistent trouble falling asleep before big deadlines, talk with your doctor about recommending some sleep therapies or medications.

> Did you know that more electrical impulses are generated in one day by a single human brain than by all the telephones in the world? No wonder E.T. wanted to phone home.

# ON THE CATWALK

I promised a free review, so here you go.

1. **Give myself some space.** This will help me to form good study habits and be more efficient with my time.
    - **Decide on a time and place** so my brain knows it's time to work.
    - **Have necessary materials close by** so I don't waste time.
    - **Eliminate as many distractions as possible,** so I can get the work done faster.
    - **Dress for the occasion** and change into study clothes that signal "work"—I'll save the yoga pants for afterward.
    - **Keep my goals where I can see them,** so I can fight the urge to procrastinate and feel the thrill of success.
2. **It's all about timing.**
    - **I win a prize** every time I meet a short-term goal that takes me closer to my long-term goal.
    - **Take a break** every twenty to thirty minutes so my brain doesn't go comatose. My dog is starting to look at the door longingly.
    - **Pace myself** by keeping a monthly planner so I can get work done early instead of freaking out about deadlines.
3. **Be realistic and stay positive** about how much I am actually able to accomplish so I'll work with more drive and less drag.
4. **Catch some Zzzzs** and keep to a healthy bedtime so that my brain has time to sort and review what I've just studied.

THE DEADLINE DAREDEVIL

# How to Shrink-Wrap Your Brain

**4**

## Study tricks your friends will beg you to tell them

I'm no telepathic genius, but I'll bet that if I visited your desk to check out your study aids you'd have pencils, pens, paper . . . and maybe index cards, if we're lucky. If that's true, your desk needs a serious makeover. The index cards have some potential, I'll admit, but good studying (as we learned in the last chapter) requires engaging your brain. A drawer full of boredom will hardly do that.

If *I studied all night and still failed the test* is your mantra, this chapter is for you. Many of my students would come to me after I handed back their test grades, chanting this very same mantra while looking like someone had just stolen their breath. If I probed to find out what "studied all night" meant, most would admit it had something to do with opening the book and staring at the pages for hours, hoping the information would miraculously carve its way into their brains. Of course, you already know why this "study" technique didn't work: Input but no Output.

Think about what catches your attention every day—bright billboards, fast-paced commercials, and just about *anything* on a television screen. Some pedagogists ponder why so many Americans under twenty-one can recite five beer slogans but not the first five presidents of the United States. My response is this: when was the last time you saw John Adams and James Monroe running along a beach with bikini-clad pilgrims? I mean, that's the sort of image you'd remember, right? Marketing executives are no fools. They know the tricks that get people memorizing worthless jingles for plastic cheese and colored fruitless juice. So, what do they know that we don't?

The marketing folks know this: **some combination of color, movement, sound, and mnemonics will make virtually anything memorable.** Let's apply that to the topic at hand and see what we can do about giving your desk drawer a face-lift.

Oh, and since you already know your primary learning strength from chapter two, I've added 🎧 for Auditory, 👓 for Visual, and ✋ for Kinesthetic beside the study tricks to give you a starting place depending on your primary learning strength. I'll also include a series of icons to guide you to quick study tricks when you're short on time ⏱, tricks that are great for groups 👫, tricks that work best when you're on your own 👤, tricks that require extra materials ✂, and tricks best paired with chocolate 🍫. Maybe not that last one, since isn't everything better with chocolate?

Of course, don't take my icons as gospel truth. Just because you may be a ✋ doesn't mean you won't like Tinted Tabs (which I marked a 👓). Nearly all learners use at least a little bit of each strength, so the learning strength notes are simply a suggested starting point as you begin testing out tricks. And, just because you're home alone doesn't mean you shouldn't give Twisted Twister a whirl. Even though it's listed with a group icon, it may be the best thing you've ever done to prep for your vocab test, and if so, go for it. This should go without saying, but just in case it isn't obvious, feel free to customize the tricks to stimulate your own strengths and interests. For example, I said Paper Flaps fit all three strengths because if you're an Auditory learner you can speak aloud whatever is on the cards, if you're a Visual learner you can simply stare at them and cover the flaps to test what you've seen, and if you're a Kinesthetic learner you can flap and flip while you practice. The point? *Make these tricks work for you.* On a final note, if your school has begun to incorporate e-textbooks (lucky you!) you have a unique toolbox available to you as you study in addition to what is listed here, and much of this will be tweakable and applicable to your system.

# Color

The next time you're near a market, grab some colored pencils, pens, or markers. If you think color is only important for Visual learners or kindergartners, you are mistaken. Unless you see the world in monochrome and prefer it that way, a little bit of color is just what the doctor ordered to spice up your study life and help improve your learning efficiency. Here are a few ways to incorporate color into your notes and (assuming you've purchased them) into the margins of your books.

**RAINBOW NOTES** are an art form using color to denote new information. The key is finding the balance between too much and not enough so that you are effectively marking the most critical ideas, terms, or developments in the plot as they appear. Get started by jamming a couple of colored pens into your backpack and the next time the teacher starts spouting off terms you've never heard before, you're ready to write them in red and look them up at home later. Once you've looked up the definitions, you can write them alongside in green. Outline major ideas you want to remember in orange (unless of course you prefer purple). Use as many colors as you like to both take and interact with (that is, study) your notes, creating as many color-coded categories as are helpful for you. **In addition to getting you actively involved with your notes,**

it will also create an easy identification system so you are able to scan your notes quickly and spot bold terms as they apply to themes or new concepts. (🎧, 👓, 👊, ☝)

**ENTERTAINING UNDERLINING** uses colored pencils or markers to represent your responses. Just as with the Rainbow Notes, **create your own key and try to be consistent from book to book and subject to subject (where possible) so you are able to develop your own language of note-taking that you can easily reference for years.** Your color key might start off like this: red underlining means "this is the most moronic idea I've ever heard"; purple means "this is absolute genius, and I'm having it tattooed on my right forearm"; yellow means "this is a critical moment/character introduction for the story, I just know it!"; and orange means "huh?" so you can ponder the point later or ask someone else her perspective. Entertaining Underlining will save you bundles of time because you won't have to take notes while you read or stop and make comments in your margins every single time you underline, but you'll have the benefits as if you did. They are also handy because the book becomes full of color-coded notes at the ready for when the teacher asks some obscure question about Piggy's glasses in *Lord of the Flies*. Of course, you will have brought your vividly noted book to class and will be able to flip quickly and find the yellow-coded answer, impressing the lovely person next to you while the poor saps in class are still frantically flipping through 150 pages of meaningless penciled underlining. (👓, 👊, ⏰, ☝)

**TINTED TABS** help organize your notebook and will save your bacon if you're using a single notebook to hold multiple types of notes from one class, or multiple sets of notes from different classes. There is nothing more frustrating than knowing *my notes are in here somewhere* but not being able to find them for your second period teacher's pop open-notebook quiz. To save yourself such pain, devise a system where colors represent certain categories and then mark the appropriate color as a check or scribble in the top right corner of your notes. For example, in your lab book mark blue in the corner for the pages that included dissections, red in the corner for the labs where you studied chemical reactions, and purple in the corner for notes you took preparing for the labs. Or, if it's a literature notebook, assign a color to each of the novels that you read for the course, like green for *Gone with the Wind* and blue for *To Kill a Mockingbird*, so that on the days you discuss one or two novels you can find the notes with a quick flip. **Not all of the pages will need to be or should be color-coded—only the ones you think are most critical.** Once you get the most important corners marked, the only thing left is to make sure your lab book doesn't end up in your literature class. (∞, ⏰, 🥄)

**DOODLING DIAGRAMS** don't require any artistic skill and will help your brain see what you are learning from a fresh perspective by doodling with a purpose. With a handful of markers or colored pencils at the ready, flip to a blank sheet of paper in your notebook and begin to organize what you have just learned in class today into some sort of picture. If you're studying physics, draw Newton and his falling apple, and be sure to make relevant notes on the doodle about what you have learned (such as the velocity of the falling apple as a result of gravity, or the deceleration of the apple as it rolls down the hill away from the tree). Science and math pair well with diagrams, but that doesn't mean you need to leave out the softer subjects. It will take a whole lot of branches to keep track of the marriages of Henry the VIII as a family tree. Or, keeping with the tree theme, you might look at Boo Radley's tree in *To Kill a Mockingbird*, and sketch the gifts inside that represent major themes in the book, drawing parallels to what you've learned about the characters. The point is to put your doodles to good use—just because it's homework doesn't mean it can't be pretty. (∞, ✊, ❗)

**CONSTRUCTIVE CONSTRUCTION PAPER** is an easy win when you don't have a lot of time to doodle and make paper cutouts to study, but you want a clean, simple solution for reviewing something every day so you'll still know it in a few months when finals roll around. Grab your kid sister's construction paper (perhaps asking first, you don't want to make her cry) and pick out a few sheets of bright colors, each different. (Different colors keep this exercise interesting for the brain.) For the sake of example, let's say you have five equations to memorize, a short set of historical dates, and a passage out of Macbeth. Using a different color for each subject, write out each on the construction paper with a permanent

> Your brain is potentially larger than Albert Einstein's, since the average brain is 3 pounds and his weighed a minuscule 2.71 pounds. Maybe size doesn't matter that much after all.

black pen. Tape your equations on the wall next to the toilet (no joke—now you know why I suggested permanent marker), your Macbeth passage next to the sink where you brush your teeth, and your historical dates in the kitchen where you fill your water glass. The colored paper will automatically draw your eyes to the card every time you brush your pearly whites for two minutes. (If you want extra sticky stars, and if the topic bears a lot of review, get the paper laminated and hang it in your shower or tape it to your kickboard when you swim laps at the pool.) Congratulations. You've just made excellent use of Dead Time while polishing your gleaming smile, and you may even have given your little sister a head start on the Quadratic Formula. (∞, ✊, ✏, ⊘, ❗)

These are just five possibilities of how color can make studying easier (not to mention cheery). Test them out. You will probably discover even more ways to use color in the process.

# Movement

A little less gawk and a lot more action should be the motto of everyone's study hour. There's a smidge of Kinesthetic learner in all of us, and we would do well to get a bit more involved with what we're learning. What this means is that instead of staring at a page and expecting the information to become burned into your conscious memory, force yourself to get mobile while you study and to make use of Dead Time you might have spent aimlessly waiting for the bus or the orthodontist.

**FLASH CARDS** are a timeless wonder and are more amazing than you may think. If there are formulas, definitions, or key themes you need to remember, this is an effective little tool to give your brain practice. And it's cheap. Flash cards are terribly underestimated because they're just simple index cards. But, they're easy to use, inexpensive, and highly portable. Both the act of organizing your notes onto the cards and practicing them are productive Output. Even more effective is designing a question-and-answer quiz that flips front to back so you can test yourself as opposed to only listing the information on the front. This works for non-Q&A info as well, such as quotes, since you can put one-half of the quote per side and quiz yourself about the part of the quote that is missing. Even equations work. Put the variables on one side (Force, Mass, Acceleration) and the equation on the other ($F=MA$). **Putting a minimal amount of information on each flash card (as opposed to printing the world's smallest version of the Constitution on a single card) will make the "flash" that much more effective.** So, the next time you have an unexpected wait in line or a long red light, pull out your cards and flash yourself. (🌓, ᴏᴏ, ✊, ⏲)

**PAPER FLAPS** are a cousin to flash cards, but with a slightly higher risk of paper cuts because of all the excitement. Flapper, beware. To make one, fold a piece of paper in half lengthwise, with the right half of the paper falling short of touching the left by an inch or two. On the left-hand side of the fold write key battle locations in the Civil War. Now open the paper and on the right-hand side of the fold write *very brief notes* of why that battle was important, such as where it was located, or casualties, or who won. Once you have filled both sides of the paper with information, you can play "peek-a-boo" with your brain by looking at the left-hand side of the paper, trying to guess the answer, and then lifting the flap to see if you got it right. The trick is to leave enough space between each line so that you don't see the answer to the next question before you've asked it. (🌓, ᴏᴏ, ✊, ⏲, 🖐) (See page 106.)

**MEMORY FANS** require a bit more preparation, but for the origami enthusiast this is a real winner of a way to study. First, fold a piece of paper back and forth multiple times, as though you were going to make a folded fan to cool yourself on a humid day. The tinier the folds, the more statistics, definitions, and events you can include. On the first flap, write a question, word, or date you are supposed to know. Behind that flap, write the answer. Do this for all of the flaps until the paper is full. You might even tape both ends of the paper together to make a tube so you can study by flipping it around your fingers, kind of like a corrugated toilet paper tube on its hanger. Lovely image, eh? The nice thing about this device is that you can use it backward and forward, not to mention it keeps you cool during heat waves. (🌓, ᴏᴏ, ✊, ⏲, 🖐)

**TWISTED TWISTER** may be the strangest way you have ever studied, but at least you're guaranteed a good workout and, potentially, fun with friends. Get a pack of colored index cards and pick two different colors for this game, such as green and orange. On all the green cards, write the word, date, or compound you are trying to learn. On all the orange cards, write the answer. Do this for at least twenty-four different pieces of information and then spread them out on the floor randomly, but in four even rows. Turn on your favorite tunes (preferably without lyrics so your subconscious can stay focused) and get your feet moving. Put your right foot on a random green card and look for its match, placing your left foot on it once you find it. Hold that pose. Now use your left hand to pick a random orange card and match it with your right. Without moving your hands, pick a new green pair for your feet. If your study group is studying multiple subjects together, you can use this as a review strategy and organize subjects within their own color of index cards: red for literature, green for history, orange for chemistry, and so on. This may not be the next big seller at Christmas, but it's sure to be a hit at your next study group. Even if you play the game alone, you're guaranteed to stay awake while you study. (🎧, ᄋᄋ, ✊, ⛏, ✎)

**OLD MAID IN THE SHADE** is a method that uses the same supplies as Twisted Twister. In fact, if you're breathless from your first round of Twisted Twister, you can take a break and use the same cards for this game. Or, if the Twisted Twister cards have been decimated, use your Flash Cards. This game requires a few extra hands and brains, so get your study partners together for this one. Deal out the index cards as you would a deck of cards and play a round or two of Old Maid or Go Fish (or Memory, if you're by yourself). This is especially great for learning vocabulary. For instance, if you have "cuchara" in your hand, you can ask if someone has "spoon" (which is what *cuchara* means in Spanish), make the match, and get a point. Of course, games like these are a bit more fun if there is a prize at stake. How about the loser buys a round of smoothies? (🎧, 👓, ✊, ♨, ✎)

**MAD ACTOR** is for those who have an imagination and don't mind acting a little crazy for the sake of an education. This study trick can be performed with or without study partners. If there is a scene in a piece of literature you don't understand, or if you're trying to remember a historic decision, act it out. Pretend you're Galileo defending himself before the courts, saying you are not heretical by believing the world is round, and act out what the bantering must have sounded like. Props, costumes, and various stances around the room will make this even more memorable. If it's chemistry, pull out your test tubes. If it's physics, get marbles, levers, or pulleys to work for you. If it's biology, act out microevolution as you change from one creature to the next. **If your study partners are nearby, a great way to enhance this game is to turn it into charades.** Folks might think you've gone mad in study hall, but at least you'll earn an A on the test before being shipped off to a rubber room. (🎧, ✊, ♨, ✎)

**LOCATION CODIFICATION** is a fantastic method for memorizing just about anything by storing information in a secret code around specific locations in your house. It was developed way back in the day, long before some guy invented sticky notes, by Simonides—a Greek poet during the fifth and sixth centuries BC—and is often referred to as the "loci" method. Memory greats swear by this method, like the 2006 World Memory Champion, Clemens Mayer, who memorized 1,040 random digits in a half hour. The great news is that you don't have to be a memory genius to pull this off. Experts believe that a person with an average memory can use the loci method to memorize the sequence of a shuffled deck of cards in less than an hour. So, what are we waiting for?

Walk around your kitchen and pick ten "locations" where you will store imaginary information. Examples would be the microwave, the fridge, the kitchen sink, the kitchen table, and the bookshelf. Go around the room and write them down on a paper numbered one to ten. Done? Okay, let's say you need to memorize the five stages of grief for social studies class tomorrow: denial, anger, bargaining, depression, and acceptance. Start with the first location: the microwave.

The second location is the fridge, for Anger. Picture the Incredible Hulk walking up to your fridge and slamming his green fists into the double doors, ripping off the doors, and walking out of the kitchen with the refrigerator doors dangling like bracelets on his wrists. Anger.

The third location is the kitchen sink. Visualize your little sister standing next to the sink expressionless and bashing the sink to smithereens with a metal bar that keeps growing bigger and bigger as she continues to bash. Bar-gain-ing, get it?

Almost there. The fourth location is the kitchen table, and the grief stage is depression. Visualize yourself sitting at the table eating a bowl of cereal when suddenly a meteor crashes through your roof and smashes through your table, leaving a huge crater, a "depression," in your kitchen linoleum. Depression.

The last one is Acceptance, and the fifth location is the bookshelf. Visualize a line of a dozen or so ants walking across the edge of the bookshelf. Now, picture yourself pulling out a massive lumberjack axe and whacking the shelf to bits as a way of getting rid of the ants. Axe-cept-ants. Well done!

It may sound like I have a lot of pent-up rage (whaddaya mean, you think I'm angry, huh, huh, huh?!?!), but it's actually all part of the strategy. **The stranger, messier, and more ridiculous the image, the easier it will be for your brain to remember.** Now that you have the five locations filled with these five stages of grief, go around and visualize each one *three times more*—the Nile in your microwave, the Incredible Hulk at your fridge, your sister bashing the sink with a bar, the crater in your linoleum, and the axe chopping the ants to bits: denial, anger, bargaining, depression, and acceptance. As unforgettable as these images might seem, reviewing them over and over is key if you want to retain them for any length of time, so please don't skimp on that last critical step.

This technique can be used for more than just lists of words. It works for remembering historical figures, lines of speeches or poems, phone numbers, locker combinations—the possibilities are endless. To make it even easier on yourself, **use the same ten locations each time you have something to memorize; that way you only need to remember what was in the location.** If you are memorizing a list with more than ten items, fill up your "kitchen" and then move down the hall to the family room for ten more locations. Superstars of this method have developed up to hundreds of mental locations to store information; maybe you should start building yourself a mental mansion. (∞, ▮, ⊙, ▯)

Don't stop with these ideas—there are plenty more out there! The key here is *creativity*. **Don't worry about classmates thinking Flap Happy looks silly. When you're pulling amazing grades and someday making your place in the world, they'll be the first to boast that they used to sit next to you in algebra.**

# Sound

Few people take advantage of their eardrums when it comes time to study, or, if they do, they're filling them with random noise instead of study material. In the last chapter, you learned that brains like patterns; but brains also like repetition (which is why I keep repeating what you've learned in earlier chapters—I know, I know, your awe at this sort of brilliance has me fairly blushing).

**FOREIGN TRANSLATIONS** is one way to make learning another language a lot less foreign. At some point in every American's life, one should endeavor to learn—*oh no, not the f-word*—yes, a foreign language. For those of you reading this who are linguistically privileged to have lived in a non-English-speaking country or bilingual home, props to you. Regardless, this little technique should be helpful for all when it comes time to learn a new language.

Grab a handheld recorder and a pen and paper, and write down a list of sentences you are trying to learn in, let's say, German. You may think you only need to learn vocabulary words to get by, but trust me on this one when I say writing down a full sentence will make learning and using the language that much easier later on. It could be something as simple as "The kite is yellow." It doesn't have to be complicated when you're starting out. **The point is for your brain to hear how the flow of a real conversation sounds *in that language*, since that's the ultimate goal of learning a language—having a conversation.**

The second step of this best-case scenario is that you are able to find a native German speaker nearby. If you can't find a native speaker, track down your teacher or a German foreign exchange student or someone who speaks German with relative authenticity. Ask the speaker to read the sentence aloud into the recorder at a normal speed *three times*, pausing for a moment between each repetition. After he has repeated that sentence three times, speak into the recorder giving the translation of what he said *once*. Do this for all of the sentences that you wrote down and thank the speaker very much. That's the easy part.

The even easier part is plugging in headphones and pressing play . . . repeat, play . . . repeat, play . . . repeat, play. When you're eating breakfast, waiting for the subway, walking through the mall, play . . . repeat. After hearing the sentences a dozen times, try to say the sentences *with* the recording. If you're afraid you'll look crazy, just mouth the words. (Or, better yet, hang a sign around your neck that says "not crazy" and speak even louder. If nothing else, it will guarantee you a seat on the subway.)

An American friend of mine lived in Korea for a couple years and hailed this technique as the best way to learn a language since sliced kimbap. She didn't speak a word of Korean when she moved there, but after a short time using Foreign Translations she found that Koreans complimented her frequently on the authenticity of her pronunciation: a taxi driver was stunned by the obviously American girl asking him in perfect Korean to please take a left at the next intersection. She said the expression on his face was hilarious, very "deer in the headlights" . . . except from the other side of the steering wheel.

> An eternity from now, in the far distant future when you turn 30, your brain will shrink a quarter of a percent in mass each year, losing about 7,000 irreplaceable brain cells a day. Go sudoku puzzles!

Foreign Translations is an excellent tool for learning a foreign language because it will help you learn the syntax, pitch, and rhythm of a language alongside vocabulary *simultaneously*. Most foreign language CDs only give the foreign sentence once and then the definition (to save on space, most likely), but this is *far less effective* than the repetition method of stating the new sentence three times. Your brain needs new things repeated with great frequency to really get it, so it's critical that you hear a new piece of information at least three times before moving on to the next piece of information, especially if it involves your tongue learning to do somersaults in a whole new language. And, the best news of all? If you can talk your classmates into Foreign Translations, each of you can take a chapter and then swap recordings. Obviously, this tool is strongly Auditory. However, even if that isn't your primary learning mode I still recommend you give it a try. I've used this method myself (and I barely even score a point on the Auditory learning scale), and it's now my favorite way to learn a new language. (🎧, 🎹, ✏️, 🧍)

**THE PRICE IS CHEAP** is the name of your very own game show to success. And, it's true—the price of this game *is* cheap. Since you already have your handheld recorder from Foreign Translations, this won't cost you a dime (assuming you're using rechargeable batteries like the environmentally aware consumers we should all strive to become). The game is quite simple: Write a list of questions and answers about whatever it is you are studying. Then, read a question into the recorder, such as "What four ways does my brain learn new information?" Pause for two or three seconds, and give the answer (which of course you know to be color, movement, sound, and mnemonics). If you want a two-fer, open up your Rainbow Notes and simply read through your colorful new vocabulary words and their definitions, with the proper pauses of course so you can quiz yourself. Your Entertaining Underlining or Paper Flaps can also come in handy here. You've already done the work organizing what you want to memorize; this is just another way of getting it into your head. And when it comes to studying, variety is a good thing. Drag this recorder with you wherever you go and try to answer each question (or define each word) before hearing the answer. You may need to hit pause so you have time to give your answer before you interrupt yourself. Just don't cheer too loudly when you get the answer right; you might scare the folks in line next to you. (🎧, ✏, ⏱, 🕯)

**TECHNO TROUBADOUR** is a sure way to memorize that psalm, poem, or speech you need for class. If it's a particularly long piece, break it down into smaller chunks of one to two minutes or less so that your brain can digest it one bite at a time. (There's a reason phone numbers have a dash in the middle—our brains like taking little bites.) Give the name of the passage and its author or address, then read using *the most enthusiasm you can muster*. Go overboard. Real recording artists look ridiculous when they are laying down a track of spoken word. (I know this because I used to be one.) Try to focus on memorizing just one bite at a time and remember to review each section you've successfully memorized as frequently as possible so that your brain knows you want all the sections stored in your Long-Term Memory. For an added twist, consider swapping tapes if there are others in your class with the same assignment (something you can do for The Price Is Cheap as well). If nothing else, it will force you to make your tape sound more interesting. (🎧, ⏱, 🕯, ✏)

> Your brain is 80 percent water. Instead of complaining you feel *foggy* in the morning, maybe you should say you're feeling *soggy*.

Putting your homework on a little pocket recorder is a great way to make use of long car rides, treadmills, insomnia, or mindless tasks where you need your hands but could use something to occupy your thoughts. There are just two things to keep in mind with these sound-related suggestions. First, you need to be attentive while listening. Playing the record while you sleep will not help you learn the material and will only infuriate your roommate. (In fact, it might even cause you to sleep fitfully and wake up exhausted.)

Second, no matter how much you like listening to yourself, if you drone on in a monotone for hours you will definitely lose interest. So, *speak with enthusiasm*. If you really want to get creative (and can afford the time), feel free to add an instrumental background or sound effects that emphasize what you're learning. You can even make up a cheesy song as a way of learning random facts. Since this is a little pocket recorder, no one will hear it but you—so do whatever is necessary to learn the material. As long as your creative extras don't distract from the main point, just about anything is game!

## Mnemonics

In fourteen hundred and ninety-two . . . how come we remember the date Columbus set sail for the New World? How come we don't remember other important dates, such as the year the Revolutionary War ended, when the Mona Lisa was painted, or when the Berlin Wall fell? It's because of a sing-song rhyme, called a mnemonic. A mnemonic is a lyrical device (often using rhyme or meter) that helps the brain remember something. It's a powerful tool that has people like my mom still singing the advertising jingle for Fruit Stripe Gum nearly fifty years after she first heard it. **Rhymes get very little respect when it comes to the learning process, but they definitely play a key role in helping us find patterns in information, making new information easier to remember.** This is also why you are able to remember nursery rhymes from a decade or two ago and not necessarily your locker combination. You may find that rhythm and song work equally as well, so here are a few ideas.

**RHYME LINERS** may not seem new (since you probably already knew the Columbus example I used earlier), but I've included a couple of tips to help you make your own. Choose a date, person, or fact you are trying to remember, and write a silly sentence with a rhyming couplet (1492 . . . ocean blue). **The rhyme doesn't have to be metrically accurate or even elegant, but you do want one of the key details to be one of the rhyming words.** For instance, if the line had been *In 1492 Columbus boarded his boat, to see how far around the world his wooden home could float,* it would be much harder to remember the *date* of his discovery, which is the key detail, because our brains want to focus on the fun part that rhymes: boat and float. So, start by picking the person or word that you want to remember, and then write a phrase with that key detail *falling at the end* of the line. Next, think about what words rhyme and relate to that key detail and pick a couple to experiment with as you write the second half of the sentence. As long as the sentence helps you remember what you need, it's fair game. You should have heard the ones I came up with to remember Impressionist painters in college—terrible puns and super corny rhymes. But, they worked, I got an A, and look at me now (yes, I know . . . still writing terrible puns and super corny rhymes). (🎧, 👓, ⏰, ♒, ❗)

> Just in case you were wondering, it is not actually possible to tickle yourself. The cerebellum warns all his brainy buddies that you are about to tickle yourself and they just ignore you. How rude.

**LEARNED LETTERS** uses alliteration to help you keep track of a string of key details. At some point, an English teacher probably taught you about alliteration, but if not, don't stress. Alliteration is simply when the first letter of a group of words is the same for many of the words in a series. The words don't need to rhyme, but because they are punctuated by a repeating letter they will definitely have a rhythm. And, **having one primary letter will help you remember the important details**. Here's an example: Pope John Paul II Pleaded with Parliament to Protect Prenatal People. (The alliteration here is with the letter P, but you knew that.) Just make sure, as you did in Rhyme Liners, that the important info you are trying to remember is part of the alliteration. (🎧, 👓, 👁, 👫, 🕴)

**MEMORABLE MELODIES** borrows a memorable tune (such as the Gilligan's Island theme song, *Jingle Bells* or *Dancing Queen*), and rewrites the lyrics to fit the subject. Again, you'll want your key details to be repeated through the song to help you memorize them, but any ridiculous filler you want to add will make the learning more fun. And, nearly any time something is fun, you have a better chance of remembering it. The music will actually help you build rhyme or rhythm into what you're trying to learn, but be warned: this method is quite successful and you may remember the song for a long, long time. (🎧, 👫, 🕴)

In all you've seen, remember this: finding time to rhyme what you're learning may refine your line of thinking and make your study time primely sublime.

# ON THE CATWALK

1. There are **four ways** I can influence my memory patterns to help my brain store and recall new information.

2. **Color** gets my visual senses stimulated to learn.
   - **Rainbow Notes** are color-coded so the info jumps out.
   - **Entertaining Underlining** uses a color to underscore my reactions to what I have read.
   - **Tinted Tabs** uses a color key to mark the top corner of my notes.
   - **Doodling Diagrams** uses sketching to help me see new patterns in the information I need to learn.
   - **Constructive Construction Paper** helps me memorize equations or brief passages by posting them on colored paper in key Dead Time areas.

3. **Movement** keeps me active and alert.
   - **Flash Cards** are good while waiting in the lunch line.
   - **Paper Flaps** show a fragment of information while hiding the rest so I guess the answer.
   - **Memory Fans** help me flip back and forth between questions and answers.
   - **Twisted Twister** makes me match Q&A or vocab/definition using my hands and feet.
   - **Old Maid in the Shade** uses flash cards with games like Old Maid, Go Fish, or Memory.
   - **Mad Actor** reenacts debates or historical or literary scenes with props and costumes to help me recall events. (But there's no way I'm dressing up like William Wallace.)
   - **Location Codification** assigns outrageous clues to memory spots around the house.

4. **Sound** helps me tune in to what I'm learning.
   - **Foreign Translations** repeats each foreign sentence three times and then gives the definition.
   - **The Price Is Cheap** is a way to quiz myself using a recording of Q&A like a game show.
   - **Techno Troubadour** breaks up long passages into short chunks so I can review anytime, anywhere.
5. **Mnemonics** get my tongue doing somersaults (not to mention my brain).
   - **Rhyme Liners** puts the main idea at the end of a line and rhymes it with something so it's easy to remember.
   - **Learned Letters** uses one letter to organize and remember a group of words.
   - **Memorable Melodies** rewrites the lyrics to memorable songs so I can "sing" the answers.

**THE MACK SLACKER**

# Frequently Masked Questions

# 5

Most common ways students fail, and how to succeed

Well done, you're almost there! So far we've covered the basics of how the brain categorizes and stores information, how to make the most of your study time, and creative ways to study based on your learning style. All you have left are some tips to make student life easier, then you are on your way to genius. This chapter hosts the most common student complaints I heard while teaching college and high school students, as well as how to overcome them. Enough with the chitchat.

## "That Wasn't in My Notes"

How frustrating is it to study your notes, sit down to a test, take one look at the questions, and wonder if you're even in the right class? Very. We've all done it. (Of course, some of us *were* in the wrong class, but that's another story.) Taking notes is an art form that couples discipline with creativity, as is true with most other art forms. So, a few suggestions on how to create (and use) great notes.

**BE READY.** Very few teachers will ever begin a lecture by saying "Please open your notes to a blank page and pull out a pen with plenty of ink and remove the cap because I'm getting ready to say something important." In fact, I've never met one. It would be nice if they gave that sort of blazing intro, but they don't. Your job, then, is to assume that *everything* the teacher says is potentially important; if she's willing to repeat it seven times a day, it most likely is.

From the moment your seat hits the seat you should have your materials ready to record whatever the teacher says from word one. **If your pen is in hand and your paper is ready, you'll be amazed**

> Your brain is more active during the night than it is during the day. Maybe that explains all your "bad pizza" dreams.

**how many more important points you will notice than if you were sitting there waiting for an announcement about pulling out your notebook.** Who cares about whether or not this wins cool points. You'll never see most of your classmates after graduation anyway, and your preparedness will heft you toward opportunity and success.

**BE THOROUGH.** Everything the teacher writes on the board is important. Trust me, if she willingly risked carpal tunnel rewriting it for all of her classes, she darn well thinks it's worth your writing it down once. However, *don't just copy it.* "Electra, 1937" won't mean much come test time when you are trying desperately to remember what it had to do with Amelia Earhart's story if that's all you copied from the board. **Most of the time teachers write facts on the board to structure their lecture, not because it is all they want you to remember.** Write her explanation of each point as well as what she puts on the board so that the notes are a more accurate reflection of her lecture. Don't worry about spelling errors or sentence fragments. Focus on sketching out as many critical details from her lecture as you can, such as "circumnavigational flight, disappeared over Pacific Ocean, maybe Howland Island, never found." Very few teachers, if any, will write down absolutely everything you need to know on the board. (And, if you have one who does, buy her a really nice potted plant.) Frankly, the board isn't large enough. Whatever she writes, if she writes anything at all, is simply an outline to show you how the points connect and to show that there is some sort of structure to her diatribe. Don't let her conversational, nonchalant speaking style fool you—she means business.

**BE FAST.** As you progress in your education, taking notes will become much faster and easier. Like any other skill, practice is your BFF. Begin developing this skill now by first creating a small key of symbols you can use to speed up your note-taking for common words, such as the words below. **Just make sure your symbols don't take longer to write than the actual words.**

---

**ABRV SUGGS (Abbreviation Suggestions):**

| | | | |
|---|---|---|---|
| and | + | many/quantity | # |
| change | △ | because of | b/o |
| therefore | ∴ | with | w/ |
| about/roughly | ≈ | without | w/o |
| produces | ⇒ | | |

---

You can also design your own shorthand for words you refer to commonly in class by writing an uppercase letter or letter combination and simply circling it, such as POV in your lit notes for "Point of View." Try to keep the list as consistent as possible between classes, and if you are creating a lot of abbreviations for a particular class you should probably create a key to make review easier. Keep in mind that **this should be a tool that speeds things up, not a super-spy encoding trick** that requires you to refer to your key during class

**BE FOCUSED.** As you take notes—and this, admittedly, takes a bit of practice—try to focus on the sound of the teacher's voice and write down Thing A (that she has just said) as you continue to listen to her explain Thing B. Don't tune out Thing B just because you are writing Thing A. And, don't worry about trying to memorize Thing A as she is saying it; otherwise you won't hear Thing B and Thing C. Time to memorize is later when you are reviewing your notes at home in your stellar study outfit. Tricky, I know. Another way to think of it is that you can replay what she has said through your pen (without thinking about it too much), tuning your ears into the new information. I promise that this gets easier with practice.

## "I Never Use My Notes So It's a Waste of Trees to Take Them"

If saving trees is truly your goal, there are some inexpensive, sturdy typing pads out there that cost a couple hundred bucks and transfer data directly to your computer with a simple USB connection and no paper waste. Of course, you could always tell your parents you *need* an iPad for school so you can be simultaneously studious and environmentally conscientious. Good luck with that, by the way. However, if we are honest with ourselves, most of us who have used this excuse are not really out to save trees—we just don't want to take notes, or, more accurately, don't know how and don't use them once we do. **The whole point of taking notes is to use them, and how you intend to use**

**them determines how you should take them.** Wait, there is more than one way to take notes?

On a good day, we know that notes should fit in that pretty format of A's and B's and 1's and 2's all the way down the page, right? Not necessarily. The point of taking notes is to write down new information quickly and clearly so that you have material to study from later, rather than worrying if you have the right amount of letters in your outline. Note-taking is what you make of it, and here are a few suggestions to get you started. (Be sure and flip back to Appendix B on page 106 to see examples of each of these models.)

**ROMAN MODEL.** For those of you hoping that this means someone with shimmering hair and a tan, guess again. Roman Model may be one of the most classic methods of note-taking, but that doesn't necessarily make it the best. It uses a Roman numeral for the main topic, a letter for the subtopics, and then numbers for details, and each alphanumeric (I, II, A, B, 1, 2, and so on) starts on a new line.

Most people are familiar with this model, but since few teachers actually pre-write their lectures using this model (the prep work is unnecessarily time-consuming), it makes it tough for listeners to reorganize their notes into this format while still paying attention to the lecture. However, if you're taking notes from a textbook, this method often works great since most authors write with a structure in mind. "On the Catwalk" proves this point nicely. (See pages 85–88 and 109.)

**CORNELL NOTES.** This method got its name from a professor at Cornell University who wanted to give his students some space. What a guy. On a sheet of paper, draw a line down the center so there are two columns. In one column (use whichever side is easier depending on if you are left- or right-handed) take notes on what the teacher is saying.

The Cornell professor suggested using the Roman Model to do this, but you could also use Hash Mash if you like. He also suggested starting with a specific column, but they're your notes so do what works best for you. The other column is there for you to interact with the notes, meaning you write questions or comments you think of during the lecture or look up and define main ideas and keywords during your review later that evening. Save a full section underneath both columns to write a summary of the notes or to answer the question "What was the main point of today's lecture?" (See page 108.)

**HASH MASH.** As you can probably tell, I'm a little biased about note-taking (as we all should be), and this is my favorite way to take notes (or write a book, for that matter). Nearly all teachers will give you at least a subject heading or a topic for the material they are about to cover in a given class. Write that at the top. Then, with the very next point they make, write a hash line on the left side of your paper and whatever they said to the right of it. If the teacher is speaking from a Roman Model outline, you will be able to write headings above each group of hashes as you go along. If not, no worries. The hash marks can also be indented underneath a previous line to show that it is related as a sub-point, without feeling the constraints of assigning a letter or number to that sub-point.

Benefits of this method are that it is quick and requires little organizational thought on the part of the note-taker, which allows you to focus simply on writing down the information instead. A big drawback, however, is that once the class is over you have a page covered in hash marks with so little structure that it may be hard to see the big picture. To enhance your Output, pull out these notes at the end of the day (while the lecture is still somewhat fresh in your mind) and insert headings and whatever organization you can to help the notes make more sense.

If you really want to earn your sticky stars and exercise your Output, rewrite the notes at home so they fit into the Roman Model format and are more legible, perhaps even adding something you remember from the lecture but didn't have time to write in class—this will engage your brain to its fullest and make remembering the material (not to mention studying it) that much easier later on. (See page 109.)

**SPIDER MAPPING.** For those who like to doodle, draw, and color during class, this may become your favorite way to take notes. Write the topic of the lecture in the center of the page and circle it. Subtopics then branch off to the sides all the way around the circle like a flattened spider. Circle each subtopic and then make small spiders out of them by writing details all around each. This is a great method for getting the big picture. A drawback, of course, is that if you run out of space on the page, it requires a bit of creative "connect the dots" to flip to the next page and make it clear how the two pages connect. But, if you use unlined paper and write small with a fine-point pen, one page may be enough for a fifty-minute lecture. (See page 110.)

> Two large bananas can fuel a brain's thinking for an entire day. Hmm . . . smart study snack idea. . . .

**THE MODEL MODEL.** This has nothing to do with striking a pose, but it does have something to do with posing. First, take notes in class in any format you like, Hash Mash, Mapping, Roman Model—it's your choice. Then, once you're home, construct a Lego, toothpick, sponge, or any other kind of three-dimensional model that represents key points to remember. This method may take a bit of imagination for some subjects, but for the sciences or history it can be a big win, not to mention—dare I suggest—fun.

You won't have time to use this method daily for all of your classes, but if you are trying to digest a particularly hard concept or looking to review your notes from the quarter in a fresh, memorable, creative way, the Model Model is an attractive option. The Model Model is a super means to visualize the information in a fresh way and will challenge how well you really understand it. When I was a student I used this method to turn the periodic table (which we were studying for the quarter) into a freestanding Ferris wheel where each element had its own "car." Up until that project I hadn't fully appreciated how brilliant and interwoven the periodic table was, and in the course of designing the wheel I discovered some significant gaps in my understanding. Fortunately, I learned a lot through the process and finished the wheel with a very sound knowledge of the periodic table that paid off come finals week. To this day, it was the most fun I've ever had in chemistry—and that includes lighting things on fire. (See page 111.)

**THE ENDGAME.** This is the real money. No matter how you take notes, you'll definitely want to use this little trick I learned from a Duke professor. It's absolutely brilliant, and I don't know how I made it as far as I did without it.

At the end of the day, as part of your regular review, take however many pages of notes you have from a single class and summarize them onto one (yes, one) index card. Each subject gets its own card, so, one card for world history, one card for algebra, one card for American literature, and so on. At the end of the week you will have five cards for each class, assuming a standard schedule. As a way of studying over the weekend, summarize those five cards onto one.

Hold up, that doesn't mean you should try to *squeeze* all the information from five cards onto one (even if your writing is small enough to make you one of those artists who writes love messages on a grain of rice). Instead, distill and combine the main themes and ideas of the week. Over time you'll notice that what you learned at the beginning of the week blends and almost "disappears" into what you learned at the end of the week. Don't worry about losing information from the daily summary cards—you should file them safely in a shoe box called Round One, organizing them chronologically and by class.

File each of these *weekly* summary cards in a new box and label it Round Two, which should still be organized chronologically by class, and read through them ALL *every* weekend as you progress through the quarter. You will find that the further you get into the quarter, the easier those earlier cards seem until you feel like you don't need them anymore. The constant review will also challenge you to write only the most critical information on the card, since you know you'll be reading and rereading it.

At the end of the quarter, take all of your weekly cards for one class and summarize them onto a *single* card. That way, when midterms come at the end of the quarter, you have only six note cards to study for your six classes and a whole brain full of review you have been doing diligently along the way. Cool trick, eh? (See page 111.)

• • •

For all of these note-taking methods, it's important to continue to include color (such as with Rainbow Notes) and symbols to denote key ideas. Both will increase your note-taking speed and make studying your notes later that much more efficient.

The fundamental point in all of this is that you actually *need to study the notes later.* Real-life confession: It wasn't until I got to college that I realized the whole point of taking notes in a lecture was to study them at the end of the day. Up until then, I had reviewed months of notes when-ever midterms or finals came around, but that's about the only time I ever looked at them. Don't get me wrong; I took copious notes in class using a lot of these great color-coding and symbol methods. . ... I just didn't look at the notes for months. To this day, I'm baffled at how I managed to graduate a valedictorian or get into Stanford. I was definitely an Unperfected Perfectionist, and I wonder what I could have learned had I known how to study properly.

Sadly, I was not alone in my foolishness. For a lot of folks, taking notes doesn't help much because, once they get home, their comments are either illegible or incomplete, or both. So, they don't use them. Other than the tactile practice of writing down the information the first time (which does help a little), the notes are absolutely zero help when it's time to review.

If that was you before, hopefully it will never be you again. Now that you know how to create great notes, you should find them to be a worthwhile tool. If you plan to spend a large chunk of your life taking notes, you may want to study stenography, which uses a series of loops and swirls as a code to capture information quickly. Otherwise, give these six models a try (and tell your friends you took a model to class).

## "If What He Was Saying Was Actually Interesting, I Might Stay Awake"

Granted, not every teacher is thrilling. But then again, not every class full of students is a stellar audience either. I've seen it from both sides of the podium. While some teachers could certainly do more to spice up their diatribes—forgive me if this sounds harsh—*it's unreasonable for students to expect that class will be as entertaining as the comedic spoofs on late-night TV.*

Jay Leno has a whole team of joke artists and script writers (not to mention fashion consultants—some teachers could admittedly use some assistance there) who help him prepare all day for a seven-minute monologue and twenty minutes of interviews. Meanwhile, most high school teachers have to prep for *five* fifty-minute periods of two to three *different* classes *five times a week,* and they are working with a team of one (unless their personalities have begun to split by this point because of the stress). True, it is their job to educate us, but it is not their job to entertain us. Just think of how long it took you to prepare for that four-minute presentation you gave in history class—hours, if not weeks, right? That should give you an idea of how long it takes to create an average fifty-minute lesson plan, let alone an exciting one. That's not to let teachers off the hook—learning should be fun. But, as students, we should also strive to be active learners.

With all that said, let's go back to the original problem that—for whatever reason—the lecture feels flat and uninteresting, and as you sit at your desk you are totally fading. There are thirty minutes left in class and the test is tomorrow. . . . How will you survive?

How about scaring yourself into attentiveness: it is incredibly difficult to make up what you missed while you were nodding off in class and you could fail the exam. Did that work? No?

Okay, how about sheer embarrassment: when you drool and snore during your mid-class nap, not only will you destroy any possibility of impressing your teacher, but the girls will laugh, and the soccer player across the aisle will take a picture and text it to the rest of the team, which will tease you for weeks. No, that doesn't do it either?

I didn't think so. Here are some of my favorite time-tested ways to stay awake on the littlest sleep (or none at all!). Kids, don't attempt sleep deprivation at home. Remember those snooze-reviewing rats and leave the insomnia to the zombies.

**AVOID COFFEE.** That and all those super-sodas. I know that sounds counterintuitive, but unless you have already built a caffeine tolerance by downing an espresso every morning for some time now, **the combination of stress, sleep deprivation, and a caffeine high could backfire and make you feel jittery, hyper, and unable to focus.** Essentially, what was supposed to help you could make the problem even worse. A mildly caffeinated black or green tea is a safer bet if you need a little boost.

**SUCK ON SOME HARD CANDY.** Something sour or minty works especially well in waking your taste buds and brain. As long as you aren't smacking your lips, blowing bubbles, or tossing mini-boxes of Nerds around class, most teachers will allow it. (Of course, if candy isn't allowed the sheer stealth of containing a mouthful of hidden sweets is sure to keep you alert.) If candy is *absolutely* forbidden and your teacher will burn this book for suggesting it, or explain your dilemma to the teacher before class and see if she will allow you to chew some sugarless gum.

**YAWN AS MANY TIMES AS YOU CAN IN ONE MINUTE.** Ready, yawn. If you can't get yourself to yawn, just say the word "yawn" aloud or visualize the person sitting next to you yawning. We tend to associate yawning with falling asleep, but some scientists believe that yawning actually wakes us up. **By expanding our pharynx and larynx to yawn, we are actually allowing larger amounts of oxygen to enter our lungs, bloodstream, and brain, which in turn makes us more alert.** Scientists have observed nonhuman primates (aka, gorillas and chimps) yawning in tense, threatening situations, possibly as a way to pump themselves up for what is coming next. Even dogs yawn when they (or others around them) are stressed. So, think of it as your body's attempt to wake you up with a natural oxygen high and stretch out a big one.

As long as the teacher doesn't call on you for an answer, you should also stretch both arms high above your head as you yawn, which will expand your diaphragm even further to suck in more oxygen. Your yawns may be contagious, and you could start a trend across class. Just be sure to pat your teacher on the back on the way out of class and let him know you were forcing yourself to yawn so you could focus better on what he had to say; otherwise, he might think you're totally rude.

**PUT A RUBBER BAND AROUND YOUR WRIST.** Snap it *lightly* when you feel yourself drifting off. I know it sounds a bit masochistic, but it won't harm you (if you snap it gently) and it will sting you enough to keep you alert. If you still feel drowsy, move on to a different strategy. You don't want to bruise yourself, just wake up.

**CROCHET A BEANIE AT THE BACK OF CLASS.** No kidding, it works, especially if you're a Kinesthetic learner. If your hands are busy, you're more likely to stay awake and you'll still be able to pay attention to what the teacher is saying (assuming that you've already learned how to crochet a beanie and won't be distracted by your stitches). However, if you go this route you will want to get permission from your teacher in advance, explaining that you are still paying attention and taking notes but that you need to keep your hands busy because you had a late night of homework and are having trouble staying awake. Keep your pen and notepad at the ready and prioritize homework over your handiwork so that the teacher can see you mean business. Be prepared that he may even call on you a couple of times in the beginning to prove to himself (and your classmates) that you are paying attention. If you prove to be on task and don't distract other students, he may just let you try it again sometime. This method definitely works for me. Anybody need a beanie?

**GET OUT YOUR COLORED PENCILS AND DRAW.** As long as your sketches clearly *relate to the topic* of the lecture (and are PG rated), this should pass as an acceptable way for you to learn as well as pay attention in class. Again, keep taking notes on the side so you have something to study later beyond your version of Spaceman Spiff during the 1949 Gold Rush. Call your illustrations "diagrams" and you may even get a sticky star.

**COLOR CODE YOUR NOTES AS YOU WRITE THEM.** If illustrations aren't allowed, use your colored pencils like the Rainbow Notes we discussed earlier. Bright colors, such as orange and red, do a lot to wake up the senses, and switching back and forth between colors will keep you busy and potentially more alert. If sleeping in class is consistently an issue for you, maybe you should bring back the 1980s and purchase a lot of neon school supplies to keep your pupils blazing. Regardless, actively engaging with your notes using color will help the time pass more quickly, as well as enable you to stay focused.

**SWITCH GEARS.** If the problem has more to do with the fact that class is confusing rather than your sleep schedule, it's time to become a more active participant in class. Come to class with a list of questions you hope to answer by listening to the lecture. Consider it a treasure hunt.

How do you come up with those questions? Good question. As you read through your assigned chapter the night before, make notes about what is confusing in the chapter, jot down names you don't recognize, make a note of points you disagree with, and, after doing all this, you will have a better idea of what sorts of questions to write. Then, sit back and see what the teacher has to say about it, and ask questions as they relate to that point of his lecture. Think of it as quizzing the teacher—now that's incentive! Following along with your questions will not only help you stay focused, it will also help you learn the material faster.

**IF ALL ELSE FAILS, GO TO BED EARLIER.** I know, you have homework and deadlines and a job and lacrosse, but remember those lab rats we mentioned earlier. **If rats need sleep so their brains can remember how to find cheese, you definitely need sleep to remember your cosine functions.** Do a quick Google search on how much sleep teens need—most accredited websites seem to agree that people between twelve and twenty-four years old need a minimum of eight to nine hours a night. So, try clocking in nine hours on the pillow nightly for a week and see if it improves your ability to focus. After all, the better your ability to focus, the quicker you can get your work done (ergo, the less time you need to study). You may be sleeping more than you feel you have time for in the beginning, but eventually it will all balance out.

> There are no pain receptors in the brain, which means the brain can't feel any pain. Probably a good thing when finals week comes around . . . ouch.

While a lecture may not seem exhilarating at the outset (even the word "lecture" sounds dry, antiquated, and coma-inducing, doesn't it?), learning can be an exciting process. Smarts make you a stronger person, and being brilliant can be an absolute thrill (so I hear).

# "I Just Finished Reading a Novel and I Have No Idea What It Was About"

*Wuthering Heights* isn't exactly brain candy and may or may not be the type of book you'd choose to curl up with on a rainy afternoon. Like many authors, Emily Brontë requires a reader's full attention, and that can be enough to give anyone a headache. It's okay to feel lost for a brief section, but to feel lost for a whole chapter (or even the whole book!) is unforgivable. Before you schedule an entire week for penance, consider the following ways to keep up with your reading.

**SANITY CHECK** is simple: after you have finished a paragraph, stop yourself and ask "What did I just read?" **If you cannot answer that question, don't keep reading!** In fact, as soon as you notice that your eyes are moving down the page but you aren't registering any Input, STOP. Go back to what you last remember and start again. Sometimes I wish our brains worked like scanners, where just gazing at the page would copy it onto our hard drives. But we're more hardheaded than that, so make the time for a Sanity Check. Once you've proven (after a number of paragraphs) that you are tracking with the plot nicely, do your Sanity Check once a page instead. If you really get into the novel and feel like you're tracking easily, you might even lessen your Sanity Checks to only a few times per chapter.

**READING SUMMARIES** are a wonderful tool to get into the habit of creating—yes, *even if they are not assigned.* After reading a chapter in a novel, write a brief paragraph (very brief—just a few sentences) summarizing the key points you just read. If the chapter is naturally broken in places or is enormously long, you can write the summaries as needed within the chapter. Reading Summaries are a natural extension of Sanity Checks. You'll quickly figure out whether or not you understand why Heathcliff and Hindley in *Wuthering Heights* didn't get along. Plus, you'll have your own free version of CliffsNotes to study for the final exam as soon as you finish the book.

**PLOT LINES** are a cousin to reading summaries, and they are my personal favorite because they are so simple and yet so helpful when it comes time to review or retrace my steps if I suddenly feel lost. If you don't have the attention span to write Reading Summaries at the end of the chapter and prefer more of a skeletal outline of a chapter to a paragraph description, Plot Lines may be more to your liking. As you begin a chapter, write the chapter number or title on your notes. Then, when *something major* happens in the plot, such as a significant action or a new character or location appears, write it down. Just a little three- to five-word fragment is fine, with arrows showing the chronological order. If you are anti-linear, you can start at the center and swirl around the page as the plot continues. It really doesn't matter. The hardest thing about Plot Lines is keeping them brief, and you'll soon get the hang of that.

One of the upsides of this method is that when everyone else is wracking their brains to remember the first thing Scout found in the tree in *To Kill a Mockingbird*, you can check your Plot Lines and proudly announce it was two sticks of gum. Consider adding page numbers in your notes from time to time as well, so you can flip to the text quickly when needed.

Of course, this also works for non-literature courses. If what you are reading is more textbook than novel, outline what you read using the title headings the book *already* includes, like you see with "On the Catwalk." Within each heading, look for boldface terms and key points to put in your notes as well. Feel free to draw a big frowny face in your margins if you disagree with a particular point so you can use it later in an essay or class discussion. (See page 106.)

**ENLARGIN' THE MARGINS** is something we mentioned earlier in chapter four, but it's worth a repeat plus a little twist. Even if you don't have colored pens handy (which does help make referencing your notes much easier), use something to write in the margins of your book (preferably something other than a pencil). In the margins, use symbols or colors to mark key terms, ideas, quotes, and facts.

One other truly fundamental point (quick, make a note) is when authors say things like "First, blah blah blah, second, blah blah blah," make sure you mark the first and second points in the margin with a big number 1 and 2. Most likely, the author is leading up to a noteworthy conclusion (and he won't be putting it in bold print either). Or, he may have already stated his point and this is his proof. Either way, as you go back to review his arguments later you will have an excellent guide for tracking (and responding to) his reasoning. This will also help you provide excellent source quotes in future essays.

**LIVIN' THE HIGHLIGHT LIFE** can turn the highlighter pen into either a marvelous tool or a weapon of confusion. The trick is to use it *sparingly*. **If more than 10 percent of a page is highlighted, it is too much.** The highlighter's purpose is to help you review what is most important in a text by pulling your eyes to those few points on the page that you originally thought were key. Consider highlighting the following:

- Characters' names when they appear in a novel for the first time
- Dates you should remember, as well as what happened on that date
- Key terms and new vocabulary

- Quotes you want to remember
- Points or supportive points the author is making
- Themes as they develop, or quotes that support those themes
- Something you find disagreeable or confusing, so you can find it later to ask your teacher or study group

This list is just a place to start. Depending on the subject or book, there are many other helpful points to highlight.

**Reading is an *activity*, which means it requires that you are ACTIVE. So, don't just stare at the page; write on it.** As long as you're investing all that time on Input with a book, you may as well work on the Output and have something to show for it when it comes time to write your A+ essay.

# "I Am So Stressed I Can't Even Concentrate"

Never have truer words been spoken. Well, maybe not never, but whoever said it is right. When we get stressed, our adrenal glands start pumping hard, our blood pressure increases, our heart rate increases, and the body shifts from a resting state to what's called "fight or flight" mode, where we are ready to either put up our dukes or get the heck out of Dodge.

The level of our response varies according to how stressed we actually are, but it happens to some degree when either positive or negative stressors arise. **When your body kicks into survival gear, it shuts down the brainy side of your brain so it can focus on your senses (in case you have to duck or run).** As you can imagine, that does little good when you're sitting at a desk very aware of how the room smells and what color your pencil is but with no idea of how King Sejong influenced Korea during the Chosun Dynasty. The good news is there are a number of things you can do *in advance* to tame your adrenals so that your brain can manage the stress better and focus on your studies.

- Exercise regularly (twenty to twenty-five minutes, three times a week).
- Strive for five (that is, eat at least five servings of *fresh* fruits and veggies a day; sorry, fruity toaster pastries don't count).
- Cut out caffeine (it only adds to your chemical roller coaster).
- Get at least eight (consecutive) hours of shut-eye nightly.
- Pray or meditate.
- Play with a pet (borrow your neighbor's ferret if you have to). Hospitals have shown that patients improve more quickly after playing with cuddly animals.
- *Regularly* schedule time for activities that you think are fun (even if it's painting pottery or carving kazoos).
- Spend time with your friends (and if you don't have any, make some).
- Volunteer at a local hospital, church, or school (your life will seem a lot less worrisome when you help other people out with their problems).
- Postpone the dating game for the time being (it's just so darn stressful and complicated, and you'll find it easier to concentrate at school if you worry less about your special someone). There will be plenty of time for romance later.

> A study of one million students in New York showed that students who ate lunches that did not include artificial flavors, preservatives, and dyes did 14 percent better on IQ tests than students who ate lunches with these additives. Pass the peas, please.

Trust me. I didn't date until after I graduated high school and I still married the man of my dreams.

- Make a Time Map (see the next section).
- Form a study group (multiple brains are better than one, but make sure you follow a balanced work plan as described later in the chapter or else it may *increase* rather than *decrease* your stress).
- Make a list of twenty things you're thankful for.
- Take five really really really deep breaths (it actually releases calming hormones into your bloodstream when you do this). There, I just did it and am feeling groovy.
- Have a popsicle and think happy thoughts.

Pick one of these to work on at a time and slowly start to build new habits that will lower your stress and create a better learning environment (not to mention make life a lot more fun!).

# "I Have No Idea Where My Time Went"

If there's one thing people the world over are looking for, it's more time. Modern appliances and technology have supposedly saved us lifetimes of time, but who can find it? The best way to save time is to see where you're spending it. Check out the sample Time Map in Appendix C (page 112) and fill in the blanks to fit your own schedule. Be sure to block out non-negotiable hours, such as school (you are welcome to break it down by class periods, but it is not necessary), work, or piano lessons. This is not a day-timer in which you plan meetings and appointments (use your assignment calendar for that). This is a general Time Map of your life designed around a quarter, term, semester, or whatever axis your world rotates.

Once you block out where your time must be spent on a weekly basis, you will see windows of unscheduled time.

In those empty windows, schedule regular blocks of free time and study time, figure out the best time to run errands or shop (by all means, try to avoid peak traffic hours that will only waste time), and *decide* how much time you want to spend watching TV or YouTube. Don't just let them run away with you. For an experiment, you might avoid the TV and significantly limit killing time on the Internet for one week to see how much time it actually saves you. That will be pretty difficult initially, as **scientists have found that watching TV releases a sort of brain-numbing, relaxing hormone into the body that is largely addictive.** In fact, the longer you stare at the TV the harder it will be to turn it off, so it's better just to leave it off in the first place. Once you peel yourself away from the plasma, you may find you like having extra time to practice your didgeridoo.

The key here is that you are actively making choices about how you spend your time, so that instead of simply watching it disappear you will be deciding exactly where it goes.

## "Studying Is Boring and Lonely"

Well then, invite someone over! Better yet, scope out the people in class who are at least making an effort to meet their goals (brilliance is not as critical for this endeavor as a good work ethic) and form a study group. **About four to five people is a good size for a study group; it's big enough to divide the work yet small enough that everyone gets a chance to participate.** A well-managed study group will make the learning process a lot friendlier and, hopefully, less stressful because you aren't going at it alone. Below are some of the keys to developing a great study group, as well as a few perks to tempt you.

**ACCOUNTABILITY.** If you know that someone expects you to share your notes, you will probably pay more attention to the lecture. If you know that a group of friends is going to quiz you on material before a test, you will probably study harder. Having someone depend on you is guaranteed to push you to excel.

**GAME TIME.** Many of the study aids mentioned in chapter four work great with groups. Games like Monopoly and Trivial Pursuit are just quizzes on accounting, business strategy, and historical facts, yet Americans spend thousands of hours playing them every year. So, who's to say Twisted Twister or Old Maid in the Shade won't be a huge hit?

If you decide to give the games a try at your next study group, divide and complete as much of the work *in advance* as possible so that each of you creates a set of questions and answers that you bring to your next group. That way, when you do get together, you are ready to play (and everyone else's cards will be a complete surprise). The key with study group activities is that you do the prep in advance where you can focus with fewer distractions and get the work done more quickly. Groups that get together to write questions or create study sheets tend to be less effective. The time they spend creating the materials could have been better spent quizzing each other on the material.

**SWAP MEET.** Are you tired of your Paper Flaps, your Flash Cards, your Foreign Translations, your Price Is Cheap? If so, trade them! A study group is a great place to swap study materials because you know the other people in your group and can trust that their materials will be quality stuff. This, of course, works in the reverse as well. If you know that someone else might be listening to your Price Is Cheap, you'll probably be more thorough in researching good questions and answers (not to mention speaking with gusto), which is a win-win situation all the way around.

**PASS THE BRAIN.** Scientists have found that one of the best ways to learn something is to teach someone else. This is why it is not necessary to have the *smartest* study group members, just the most diligent. **What your comrade doesn't know, you can explain . . . and that will only make you smarter . . . and him too.** You will want to be sure that all of your members are on roughly equal footing in terms of understanding the material so that there isn't one member consistently slowing down the group. There will always be points that you think are confusing that someone else gets and vice versa, so that's not to say your knowledge bases must be identical. In fact, you're better off if your interests are diversified. There's strength in teamwork, so enjoy the give and take.

# What Makes a Study Group?

While study groups can be a really good thing, they can also be a really troublesome thing. **Groups tend to go sour when the people who join them come in with differing expectations of when and how to work,** a situation that can be especially challenging if the groupies began as good friends and don't want their study group frustrations to mar their friendship. Even more challenging is if one of the groupies turns slacker and wants the others to do his work for him. It is painful to confront a friend and even harder to ask one to leave the group. Fortunately, there are a few preventative measures you can take to ensure a healthy, successful group.

I knew of one study group that went through a full year of this worst-case scenario drama. It was a group of five students from the same class, and all of them were really nice folks. Of the five, two joined the group with the expectation that they would work as hard as it takes to get an A. Two others were willing to work but preferred to hang out and eat snacks for a good portion of the time. The fifth person joined the group hoping to get a significant amount of help because he was super busy with extracurricular activities. Can you guess how it played out?

> Every time you reminisce or ponder you create a new connection in your brain, making your brain stronger. Think how beefy your brain will be by the end of this book!

The first two did most of the work for the entire group and walked away from the process incredibly frustrated with themselves and their friends. The second two were largely unaware that there was a problem because the first two were too embarrassed to explain their frustration. The fifth one could sense that he wasn't pulling his weight, but he needed the help too much to offer to step out. The lesson in all of this? Choose your group wisely.

**If you are a Work-Until-It's-Perfect sort of person and expect yourself and everyone else to be the same, then seek out that sort of person to join your group whether she is your best bud or not.** If you are more of the I-Want-To-Study-But-Only-If-I-Have-Fun-Doing-It type, you may want to avoid study groups. Honestly. If you join a study group, you won't actually get much studying done and the hangout time won't feel that satisfying because you always have work hanging over your head. Instead, **plan some fun social events with friends and use them as an incentive to get your work done faster.** Work first; play later. If you really think a study group would help, ask a strong Work-Until-It's-Perfect group if you can join them, with the clear understanding that if they aren't satisfied with your work they can ask you to leave—no hurt feelings. You might even offer them a probationary window to test-run the quality of your work. The key is to be the only Only-If-I-Have-Fun-Doing-It in the group so that you're less likely to derail their focus.

## Only Losers Need a Tutor

If you are like the fifth guy in the story who joined the group primarily for help, don't. You're better off admitting that you're stuck and asking the counseling center to help you track down a tutor. Sometimes the anonymity of working with someone you don't know can make it easier to ask questions that you worry may sound stupid. Or, if you prefer someone who isn't a total stranger, find a person in class who seems to have the material down solid and ask her to tutor you, or ask your teacher to suggest someone. Your teacher will probably have some good suggestions of whom to ask. You don't need to worry about paying a tutor since tutoring is actually a benefit to you both. As I mentioned earlier, in the course of teaching you the material your tutor will strengthen what she knows well and will challenge what she doesn't, making her all the stronger in the subject. And, you will get smarter in the process. And, she will get to put "tutor" on her college application. Everybody wins. As for the notion that only losers need a tutor, I ask you which is the greater loser—the guy who gets low grades in class because he doesn't understand the material and won't ask for help and therefore misses out on scholarships, a college-enticing GPA, and a stronger career path . . . or the guy who asks for help, aces the course, and has options? **It's critical to keep the endgame in mind and not your peers' reactions when making choices.**

An official tutoring relationship can also be better than a study group when you're really struggling with a subject because you enter the relationship with realistic expectations on both sides. In a study group you are expected to pull your weight equally. It is unfair to your friends to join their group knowing full well that you will always be lagging behind. It will make it hard to get work done, and they may resent you for it. On the other hand, you need help. There are no gimmicks in a tutoring relationship. She knows she is there for one purpose—to help you learn. So, **if you're truly underwater in a subject, save your friends for friends and your tutor for studying.**

## Our Study Group Is Kinda Lost

Whether or not your group starts out as the best of friends is not important. That the group end on good terms is. To ensure a healthy group and a happy ending, everyone must agree on a specific agenda *in advance* so that you can get the work over with as efficiently and quickly as possible. Figure out a start and stop time and a general idea of how you want to pace the meeting. For example, your biology study group could meet in the library and start at 4 p.m., cover general confusions from the past week's classes, share ideas for the upcoming individual mitosis projects that are due, swap study cards, quiz each other for next week's test, and then end at 5:30 p.m.

While the schedule could vary slightly from week to week, you could create a general outline that you are able to follow every week to keep the group on track. In fact, just to be sporting, I'll include one in Appendix D (page 113) to get you started. You might even schedule a snack and hangout time at the end to reward yourselves when you are done, since invariably that will happen and you may as well have a time set aside for it. An important note here, though, is that you'd be wise to save the party for afterward when the work is out of the way so no one has the unpleasant job of being the buzzkill who has to drag everyone back to work.

When you are in the earliest planning stages of your group, determine where you'll meet, when is a good regular time for all, and what specific subject(s) you'll study. Estimate how many hours a week each of you wants to put into this group. Finally, lay out a few guidelines defining The Ideal Study Group Member so that you all have something to aim for and everyone knows up front what will happen if someone turns slacker. Do all this *up front* over lunch so that everyone walks into the first meeting understanding clearly what to expect of others and what will be expected of them. **If designed well, a study group can be a valuable use of your time and can even develop into great friendships down the road.**

# ═══ ON THE CATWALK ═══

This is by far the longest chapter, which means you're feeling super happy right now that the notes are all written out for you.

1. **"That wasn't in my notes . . ."** because I didn't know how to take them—but I do now.
   - **Be ready** *before* class starts.
   - **Be thorough** by writing down whatever the teacher writes *as well as my own explanation of what she said while she was writing.*
   - **Be fast** by creating symbols that will fill in for concepts to make note-taking faster.
   - **Be focused** and practice writing what the teacher said while listening to what she is saying.
2. **"I never use my notes so it's a waste of trees to take them."** Or so I thought. I didn't understand my notes so I never used them, but now I have six new ways to take notes.

- **Roman Model** is the traditional I, II, A, B, . . . for taking notes on a book and for lectures.
- **Cornell Notes** uses two columns, taking notes on one side and writing comments on the other, leaving room for a lecture summary at the bottom.
- **Hash Mash** puts the title up top and hash marks down the left-hand side with notes as I hear them.
- **Spider Mapping** looks like a spider reunion on paper and gives a big-picture idea of how two concepts connect.
- **Model Model** takes the notes I copied in class and builds a structure using sponges or toothpicks as examples of key points. Save to review for finals.
- **The Endgame** requires thought, but that's the point. I summarize the notes from each class onto an index card, and at the end of the week I collate them all onto one card. At the end of the quarter, I'll distill everything onto one card, SAVING ALL THE OLD CARDS.

3. **"If what he was saying was actually interesting, I might stay awake. . . ."** That, or I could give my brain new ways to focus instead of hoping class will be entertaining. Tips for staying awake:
   - **Avoid coffee** and all caffeine.
   - **Suck on sour hard candy** or a mint.
   - **Yawn** as many times as I can in a minute to oxygenate my bloodstream.
   - **Put a rubber band on my wrist** and snap it (lightly!).
   - **Crochet a beanie at the back of class** or knot a hemp bracelet (with the teacher's permission, of course).

- **Using colored pencils,** draw illustrations of the lecture topic.
- **Color code my notes as I write them.** Nuff said.
- **Switch gears** by bringing a list of questions to class from last night's reading and quiz the teacher.
- **If all else fails, go to bed earlier.** Oh, all right.

4. **"I just finished this novel and I have no idea what it's about . . ."** because I *didn't* do the following five things:
   - **Sanity Check** is a pause at the end of each paragraph, page, and chapter, to confirm understanding of what I just read.
   - **Reading Summaries** briefly summarize the plot or the general concept in writing.
   - **Plot Lines** are a skeleton of the chapter, great for noting new terms or major developments in the story.
   - **Enlargin' the Margins** jots notes on the page, if I own the book, using colors or symbols to represent my responses.
   - **Livin' the Highlight Life** notes important quotes, dates, terms, or what's confusing or debatable, if I own the book.

5. **"I am so stressed I can't even concentrate. . . ."** My brain has shut down my ability to learn because it thinks I need to fight or fly. I can reduce stress and refocus my brain with tai chi, a grape popsicle, and walking Sparkie.

6. **"I have no idea where my time went. . . ."** I make a Time Map and reshuffle my schedule so I have work time, study time, family time, and hangout time.

7. **"Studying is boring and lonely. . . ."** so I'm going to invite specific people to form a study group. We will discuss and agree on the purpose, logistics, agenda, and expectations for the group before we make it official.

- **Accountability** provides the extra push to do my best.
- **Game Time** looks for ways to learn together and have fun doing it.
- **Swap Meet** trades study props.
- **Pass the Brain:** helping someone else learn the material will make me smarter.
- **What Makes a Good Study Group** requires the right motives, the right game plan, and the right people mix.
- **Only Losers Need a Tutor** is better than a study group if I'm super lost.
- **Our Study Group Is Kinda Lost** but if we have a clear game plan, we are more likely to succeed.

# Caution: Potential Land Mine Ahead

**6**

## Overcoming (versus overlooking) learning disabilities

No matter how hard we work, no matter how brilliantly we create, **no matter how smart we are, sometimes there are obstacles that get in the way and keep us from reaching our potential.** These obstacles are actually more like land mines, to be totally honest, because the reason they trip us up is that we don't know they're there.

Land mines? I'm talking about learning disabilities (LDs).

I know, you're probably thinking special ed class and that this doesn't apply to you, but experts tend to agree that anywhere from 6 to 10 percent of students have a learning disability, otherwise called an LD. That's as many as three students in your average-sized English class who have an LD—and many of them don't even realize it.

Read this chapter whether you think you have an LD or not and you may just learn something that will help you or someone you care about. This chapter simply covers the basics, so if you'd like further resources on the topic I've included a list of suggestions in Appendix D or you could start by looking up articles by Ann Logsdon online. Ms. Logsdon is a school psychologist and a special education administrator who has been supporting students with learning disabilities for fifteen years, and she provided some great input on this chapter.

# What Do Whoopi Goldberg, Albert Einstein, and Tom Cruise Have in Common?

When the topic of learning disabilities comes up, folks tend to flash on images of severely disabled children or frightening mental institutions. Am I right? The thing is, LDs have very little to do with intelligence or sanity (though you do have to score an average to high intelligence to have an LD). And, if you try to ignore the fact that you have one it may make you feel a little nuts.

Let me say that again, because this is a really important point: **experts believe that people must have average or higher intelligence to be diagnosed with an LD.** Some even think the presence of an LD is the result of a unique brain structure. Put differently, that means teachers and parents typically discover that a student has an LD because she is too smart to be struggling this much in a particular subject.

Many great creative thinkers, performers, athletes, and leaders have had learning disabilities and have been able to succeed despite them. (Or, perhaps, *because* of them.) It's true, and I'll prove it.

- Albert Einstein, who laid the groundwork for quantum physics, explained the theory of relativity, and answered the question "Why is the sky blue?" didn't speak until he was four, didn't read until he was nine, and failed his first college entrance exams.
- Whoopi Goldberg, who is one of ten people in the world to be awarded an Emmy, a Grammy, an Oscar, and a Tony,

and for a period in the 1990s was the highest paid actress of all time, is dyslexic.

- Walt Disney, yeah, the guy who created Mickey Mouse and Disneyland and sprinkled pixie dust over the entire entertainment industry, was labeled "uncreative" and "slow" in his early years, as well as being dyslexic.
- Winston Churchill, who led Britain to victory in World War II, saving England from being overrun by Nazis, had multiple LDs.
- Michael Phelps, who broke the Olympic Gold Record in 2008 by winning eight gold medals in a single competition and in 2009 held thirty-seven world records in swimming—talk about focus—has attention-deficit hyperactivity disorder.
- Charles Schwab, the founder, chair, and CEO of Charles Schwab Corporation, which is the largest brokerage firm in the United States—cha-ching!—did it all with dyslexia.
- Agatha Christie, an author dubbed the "Queen of Crime," who wrote more than eighty detective novels and is considered one of the most influential mystery writers ever, actually had dysgraphia, of all things.

These are just a few of many famous success stories among even more that are untold. You can't tell me those people didn't have some skills.

## I'm Confused—If You Can Be Smart and Have an LD, What Is a Learning Disability?

**A learning disability is basically having a unique way that the brain manages the Input or Output process.** Students with LDs might have difficulty fully understanding new information, integrating information (how am I supposed to take equations from math class and apply them to a chemistry experiment?), organizing information (I can't organize my notebook, let alone understand the order of mitosis), or storing information for the long term (yeah, good luck remembering what I studied all last week for tomorrow's test). Some people with LDs can get the information into their brains but they have trouble getting it out again, where organizing their thoughts on paper in essay form or giving speeches (especially in a time-stressed environment) might make them draw a total blank.

There are multiple kinds of learning disabilities, some more severe than others. The folks at Learning Disabilities of America suggest that a few common LDs you might have heard of before are:

- Aphasia: difficulty understanding spoken language
- Dyscalculia: difficulty understanding how numbers work in math, rules, or games
- Dysgraphia: difficulty converting thoughts into writing (which makes Agatha Christie's ability to overcome this LD with eighty novels a notable achievement)
- Dysphasia: difficulty processing language, such as in reading comprehension
- Dyspraxia: difficulty with motor coordination
- Dyslexia: difficulty reading words in their proper order
- Attention-deficit hyperactivity disorder: difficulty focusing or controlling both attention and behavior

And there are numerous other LDs beyond these with even longer names.

Let me also say this before we get much further—are you listening?—*all of us* struggle with what we're learning at some point in time. **It is a**

**natural and normal part of the learning process to feel frustrated by new subjects or skills, and it's that struggle that actually makes us smarter and stronger.** Honest. Scientists have found that the additional effort required to master a task or concept actually strengthens our problem-solving abilities as well as our memory.

It's analogous to a chick hatching from an egg. If you've never watched a chick hatch, look it up on YouTube. It looks exhausting, especially in real time. The poor, slimy, bedraggled-looking creature appears to be working itself to death for hours just to break itself out of an eggshell. If you've ever watched it in person, you know how hard it is to restrain yourself from reaching down and breaking the shell just to free the pitiful thing. But you can't interfere. The mental and physical skills the chick uses to get out of the egg are exactly what it needs to survive its first few weeks of life. If you help break the shell, the chick may die prematurely.

> Laughing at a joke requires five different areas of the brain to work together—yet another reason to love Bill Cosby reruns.

Humans are far more complex than baby chickens. Just ask your parents, who've been watching you break through the shell of your personhood for years.

All that's to say, just because you have struggled at some point in an academic subject or a skill of coordination does not mean you have an LD. However, if no matter how hard you struggle with one of these areas you feel like you are making no headway in cracking the shell, you may have a learning disability.

It's worth checking out if any of this sounds at all familiar. The worst thing about an obstacle is tripping over it because you didn't know it was there. Once you see it, you can hurdle it. Read on, I'll tell you how.

# You Might Have a Learning Disability If . . .

Below is a list of possible symptoms you might recognize in yourself if you have an LD, but it's by no means an exhaustive list. Keep in mind that there is no magic number of how many of these symptoms a person needs in order to qualify. A diagnosis depends more on the combination and seriousness of each, which requires professional analysis. While we all, at some point, have been challenged by some or all of these, **what waves the yellow flag that it might be an LD is if a student continues to have learning problems in a specific area that do not improve with effort and time.**

As you read the list, a general rule of thumb is that if you have only one or two of these traits (and you don't think they are really that bad), you probably don't have an LD. But, it doesn't hurt to follow through by talking with an academic counselor if you're concerned. Who knows, some of your challenges in class might need more than just elbow grease. What a relief.

Experts, such as Ann Logsdon, remind us that someone with a learning disability has average to above average intelligence and may show some of the following signs:

- Makes lots of careless errors even though "I knew the right answer"
- Has difficulty improving grades even with persistent effort over time
- Has difficulty remembering and following instructions unless they are repeated often
- Has consistent difficulty spelling
- Has poor handwriting

- Has difficulty retaining focus for an amount of time that seems normal to others
- Reads slowly or inaccurately
- Has difficulty memorizing multiplication tables
- Has difficulty with math with little to no success in any area
- Has difficulty recalling what has been studied recently
- Has difficulty putting thoughts onto paper
- Has difficulty remembering something read or heard
- Has a low self-esteem or feels frustrated with academics
- Has difficulty organizing a problem or project
- Has trouble adjusting to new settings
- Has trouble with open-ended questions on tests
- Has difficulty summarizing
- Pays too little or too much attention to details
- Works slowly

If after reading this list you recognize enough of these traits as your own, definitely track down someone experienced in learning disabilities to ask for help. On a side note, **it's generally better to talk with an academic counselor than a teacher about whether or not you may have an LD because of the counselor's training and access to resources,** unless that teacher is specifically trained in diagnosing and working with students who have LDs.

Sometimes students are easier to diagnose because their challenges are external—they work slowly, have difficulty reading aloud, have difficulty sitting still or maintaining focus—and that makes their LD more obvious and sometimes easier to monitor. Phil is a great example of this, who told me once that he thought school was invented purely to torture him.

All I knew of Phil before I met him on the first day of class was that he had an IEP (an Individualized Education Plan for his learning disabilities), and so I arranged the seating chart to make sure he was at the front of the class where I could track his progress easily. He was a fairly quiet student, answering if he was called on but rarely volunteering information. He came to class dressed in baggy pants, a t-shirt, chains, and a pencil stub behind his ear, holding a spiral notebook and, eventually, a smile. He seemed a pretty straightforward guy.

By the end of the quarter, Phil was making low B's in my low-level English class, was fairly easygoing, and didn't stick out much on my radar. I made it a point as a teacher not to investigate any of my students' disciplinary history until I had gotten to know them because I wanted to start out assuming the best and give them a clean slate to live up to those expectations. So, I actually knew relatively little about Phil outside of what I had seen in my classroom.

It wasn't until a school counselor came to my room after hours one day, wanting to know what was going on with Phil and why he got a B first quarter, that I realized something exceptional was happening. I started to pull up grade charts to show Phil's progress to the counselor, a little surprised at first that a counselor would show this much interest in a B student. It turns out Phil had been getting F's in every other class since he came to our school two years ago and was nearly expelled after throwing a chair out of a window and threatening to beat up a teacher *to his face* in another class.

In all classes but mine, the counselor went on to explain, Phil was aggressive and a class clown. He made inappropriate jokes, broke school policy on a weekly basis, and was starting to gather his own fan club of delinquent followers. I never would have guessed. Phil? Phil Williams?

Essentially, the counselor had come to my room to see if I was either bribing Phil with good grades in order to keep him in check or doing something his other teachers could implement in their classes. I really didn't know what to tell him. I had plenty of proof to show that Phil had earned his grades, so there was no trouble there. But I wasn't honestly sure where to attribute the change. Was it that I had implemented his IEP from the start without waiting for signs of trouble? Potentially, though that's something all teachers are required to do, so I can't think it was an exceptional move on my part.

Was it seating him in the front row of class? Students often underestimate that those are the best seats in the house, and at one point there were **preliminary studies showing how seating charts corresponded with grades, with a lot more A's toward the front of the classroom.** Once I got to know my students after the first few weeks, I would rearrange the seats to buffer students with IEPs by placing them next to students who were less distracting. So, it could have been the seating chart, though again that's something I'm sure his other teachers tried.

I've reflected on Phil's case many times over the years, trying to answer that counselor's question. Not knowing any of his other teachers, the only potential change I could think of was that I gave Phil a fresh start. Honestly, I think that is what a lot of us want—a fair chance. When the playing field doesn't seem fair, such as is often the case for those with learning disabilities, it makes students either explode (like Phil) or implode (like Jared).

I met Jared the first day of freshman Honors English when he slumped into a desk in the third row of class wearing all black, his fingernails even painted with black Sharpie. He looked disheveled and disinterested. I didn't know anything else about him other than what I learned over the course of that first week of school by observing him show up to class with wadded-up, unfinished homework assignments, illegible handwriting, and, other than one black pen and a single beat-up spiral notebook that he appeared to use for all his classes, a backpack filled with wadded papers. Jared was never aggressive or overtly disrespectful. If I called on him he sometimes knew the answer, but even then he liked to linger before answering. Most of the time he complained of headaches or stomachaches, seemed simultaneously stressed and bored, and did his best to show that he was out of place.

I'd like to say that I was able to even begin to understand or reach Jared like I did Phil, but I really don't think I did. I sure tried. But, no matter how I altered the lesson plans or the seating charts or my discussion and lecture style to appeal to his untapped creative side, he remained disconnected. Halfway through the year he was officially diagnosed with a learning disability, but despite my best efforts, and those of his other teachers, he remained a D student across the board. Sometimes I still find myself wondering why.

Was it his home situation? While family always plays a role in a student's development and success, I had managed to interact with Jared's parents and honor-roll older sister on a few occasions, and from what I could observe it seemed like a supportive environment. If anything, Jared's parents were as baffled as I was at how to reach him. Certainly, with his IEP in place, Jared was dealing with a more level playing field. Did I give him the same fair chance I gave Phil? I'd like to think I did, and to the best of my recollection I'm certain I supported him as best as I could. Because Jared's learning challenges were mostly internal, how well or poorly my teaching methods addressed his needs remained a mystery to me. I think Jared just wasn't interested in succeeding, unlike Phil. Perhaps his self-esteem had been shaken by having an undiagnosed LD for so long. Perhaps he was simply rebelling against his older sister's successful shadow. Whatever the reason, it was clear that Jared had made a choice not to change. Ultimately, it was his choice.

There are two reasons why I introduce these students. The first is to emphasize that **whether learning disabilities are obvious or not, they are not the result of laziness, rebellion, or other character**

**flaws. They are a genuine challenge that a student cannot simply ignore.** The second is that we all have a choice: a choice to recognize our challenges—whether they are learning disabilities or otherwise—and a choice to overcome them.

## Save Yourself Now or Pay Later: Diagnosing an LD ASAP

Unless you've attended a private high school, college is the only place you will have to pay to learn. By then, an undiagnosed LD may have made the difference between which school you wanted to attend and which schools actually sent you acceptance letters, largely because with an undiagnosed LD you are unable to work to your full potential in a traditional setting. The key is to diagnose an LD as early as possible—before you start paying for college courses that make your head swim—and to find a way to learn around it.

The second reason why I introduce these students is to emphasize that **an LD is not a death sentence to academic or financial success, just an alteration to how you learn.** Albert Einstein and Charles Schwab are proof of that. If anything, diagnosing it will make your life easier since, depending on your LD type, you can learn strategies to overcome it, get extra time on tests, get to skip oral presentations, or get free chocolate at the end of class. (Well, maybe not that last one.)

The trouble is that learning disabilities are hard to diagnose. Were it as easy as "can you roll your tongue or not" there would be no need for this chapter. Not all learning problems mean someone has a learning disability. The important thing is that **if you or someone who knows your study habits well suspects that something isn't working as it should, it's worth getting it checked out sooner rather than later.**

Ben had a learning disability that went undiagnosed until half-way through his time as an undergraduate. It's sad that it took so long for him to realize that something was off, but he says now that he just assumed all along that the struggles he faced with taking tests and studying and reading were the same struggles everyone else faced, only he got worse grades. Once Ben was diagnosed, he noticed a significant improvement in his ability to work within the university system and improve his test results. That's the good news. The bad news is he had four semesters of a mediocre GPA to turn around. So, why wasn't he tested earlier? It wasn't that his parents were inattentive (they were incredibly involved) or that his teachers were oblivious (they had simply mistaken him for a Mack Slacker), it's that his particular LD was internal and therefore not blatantly obvious. People misunderstood his attitude toward school as being the *cause* of his learning style instead of the *result* of it, and he slipped through the cracks.

> A world champion brainiac, Ben Pridmore, memorized 96 historical events in 5 minutes and a shuffled deck of cards in 26.28 seconds. Suddenly your vocab list isn't looking so bad, eh?

The great news is that **all public high schools are required by law to offer free LD testing to students if the students, teachers, or parents suspect the student has a disability.** The hitch is that public school practitioners can only evaluate students who are currently enrolled, unless the practitioner is also licensed for private practice. Most universities offer testing to their undergraduates as well, so check with your counseling department for more details. Specifically, that means telling your academic counselor "I'm having some constant, unavoidable trouble in the way I learn, and I'd like to get tested for a learning disability. I don't want to be talked out of it, I just want to get tested. Can you show me how to sign up for that?"

Trust me, even if you have to pay for the testing because you're outside the public school system, it's much cheaper than having to retake courses in college (which will hike up your tuition and slow down your career) because you didn't get the grades you needed the first time around. Another possibility, if your parents have their eye on the bottom line, is that some colleges with psychology programs offer evaluations at lower rates than private practitioners because the evaluators are actually graduate or undergraduate students who are supervised by a psychologist.

No matter who you see, if one evaluator gives you a clean report and suggests Study Method X, that's just fine—give it your best shot and see what happens. But if, after diligently working at Study Method X something still feels "off," set up an appointment to see a different evaluator. Keep asking questions until you and your parents feel satisfied with the answers.

## Please Read the Lowest Line on the Chart

It's really too bad, but some folks get all the way through high school (or even college!) feeling totally lost or stupid because they aren't good readers and can't keep track of what's happening in class—yet, they have no idea what causes them to feel that way. The amazing thing is it sometimes has nothing to do with a learning disability. It simply requires an eye exam.

Vision problems are fairly common. **If your eyes feel tired after reading only a short amount of material, if you have frequent headaches, if you read slowly or have lost all desire to read, you might need to get your vision corrected.** Sometimes poor vision in just one eye can cause these symptoms while the other eye is strong and makes it seem like both eyes are fine. Tricky little eyeballs.

If any of this sounds familiar, please oh please make the simple move to get your eyes checked. Some districts provide programs with free (or significantly discounted) eye exams, so ask both your school nurse and school counselor if they know of any. The test is painless and may even be free, and a quick read of the chart could simplify life in ways you never imagined.

# The Great News

If you have learning challenges, whether your questions are answered with a simple eye test or an LD assessment, the great news is that you have a way to get answers. **Students with learning disabilities that go undiagnosed often do poorly in subjects that are unaffected by their learning disability, simply because their self-esteem has been rattled by the frustration of an unfair playing field.** On the flip side, once they are diagnosed and begin to see improvement in their trouble areas they regain confidence in other academic areas that result in success across the board. (Because the topic of learning disabilities is more detailed than this book is able to address, I've included a number of resources in Appendix E (page 114) if you have further questions about LDs.)

The other great news is that some students with LDs who feel challenged in their academics are often incredibly gifted, creative, and passionate about other subjects. It can make for a complicated personality mix at times because, while these students are super talented, they are often perfectionists and intensely critical of themselves, any failure undermines their confidence and they reject help as a result. These complex expectations, skills, and emotions can result in exceptionally gifted students feeling as though they don't fit in anywhere. So the great news—especially if that's you—is that you do.

Perhaps it's a school club that focuses on your passion—mixed media art, anime, chess, tae kwon do, poetry, ballroom dancing—or a national organization or university summer program you can join that has annual workshops and camps—National Forensic League competitions, Sarah Lawrence College Summer Writer's Workshop, Space Camp, Stanford Camp—or a study abroad program where you learn a new language while continuing your education, such as with the Rotary Club. There are endless opportunities out there (and, yes, many have scholarships available), so make an appointment with your academic counselor for starters to get some ideas and then do some digging. Ask around. The world is your oyster, and that makes you the pearl tempered by a frustrating piece of sand.

# ON THE CATWALK

Alrighty, folks, this is the last one . . . are you feeling nostalgic?

1. **What do Whoopi Goldberg, Albert Einstein, and Tom Cruise have in common?** Not much, except that they (and many others) have LDs and have made successes of themselves despite (or, maybe, because of) them.
2. **I'm confused—if you can be smart and have an LD, what is a learning disability?** It is the brain having trouble getting new info either in or out.
   - It's not laziness or stupidity . . . in fact, you have to have at least an average intelligence to have one.
   - The challenge of succeeding with an LD will actually make me stronger, like the chick hatching from the egg.

3. **You might have a learning disability if you . . .** recognize the symptoms but ask an expert to know for sure.

4. **Save yourself now or pay later.** It's more expensive to try to get through high school and college with an undiagnosed LD than it is to diagnose it and alter my learning style, and it could cost a lot more than money . . .

   - Public high schools are required to offer testing to students for free if they request it.

5. **Please read the lowest line on the chart.** My struggles in class might not be an LD, and glasses are an easy solution.

6. **The great news** is that if I get diagnosed with an LD, I may see my grades improve and school won't be as stressful.

# CLOSING:
# What, Done Already?

I hope you have found this book helpful. If, after trying every single one of these suggestions genuinely over the next few months, you find that you are not seeing improvement, it is time for phase two.

Sit down with a parent, teacher, or counselor, and talk about why these study skills aren't working for you. There may be other issues you are unaware of that are keeping your goals out of reach.

Whatever you do, don't settle. Figure out what is slowing you down so that you can beat it. In everything you do, strive for excellence (as opposed to perfection, which is an intimidating and unrealistic goal for anyone) and then *do your best to be satisfied with your best*. That last part is often the hardest part that takes some of us a lifetime to master. Few are Nobel-prize material, but with diligence you will be a success.

# Appendix A:
# Study Tricks

## PAPER FLAPS

Questions     Answers         Open and close to
(left)       (right)            quiz yourself

| 1. _____ | a. _____ | | 1. _____ |
| 2. _____ | b. _____ | | 2. _____ |
| 3. _____ | FOLD  c. _____ | | 3. _____ |
| 4. _____ | d. _____ | | 4. _____ |
| 5. _____ | e. _____ | | 5. _____ |

→

## PLOT LINES

To Kill a Mockingbird:

Chapter Four

Scout has bad day at school
↓
Scout finds presents in tree: gum (2), Indian head pennies (2)
↓
Dill returns to Maycomb for summer
↓
Kids pretend to be Boo Radley in their skit

# Appendix B:
# Note-Taking Models

I've used the same subject—rainbows—to illustrate all the note-taking methods so you can see how the same information plays out differently in each outline.

## THE ROMAN MODEL: RAINBOWS

I. What is a rainbow?
    A. An arch of light
    B. A curved spectrum of parallel colors shining through falling water droplets either at the end of a rain shower or in a waterfall
    C. Appears in
        1. Early morning
        2. Late afternoon

II. What colors are in a rainbow?
    A. Red—ripe tomato, "stop" light, ruby
    B. Orange—tangerine
    C. Yellow—ripe banana, butter, "slow" light
    D. Green—live pine tree, fresh spinach, "go" light
    E. Blue—cloudless sky
    F. Indigo—blueberry stains on your white shirt
    G. Violet—blackberry stains on your white shirt

III. Common rainbow myths
    A. There's a pot of gold guarded by leprechauns at the end of it.
    B. Seeing a double rainbow brings you luck the rest of the day.
    C. Touching a rainbow will make you disappear—I've never heard this before. I think she made it up.

## CORNELL NOTES: RAINBOWS

1. What is a rainbow?
   - An arch of light
   - A curved spectrum of parallel colors shining through falling water droplets either at the end of a rain shower or in a waterfall
   - Appears in early morning or late afternoon

   > Look up definition of a spectrum; is that different from a prism?

   > Why is the rainbow limited to times of day?

2. What colors are in a rainbow?
   - Red—ripe tomato, "stop" light, ruby
   - Orange—tangerine
   - Yellow—ripe banana, butter, "slow" light
   - Green—live pine tree, fresh spinach, "go" light
   - Blue—cloudless sky
   - Indigo—blueberry stains on your white shirt
   - Violet—blackberry stains on your white shirt

   > Somebody's a messy eater...

3. Common rainbow myths
   - There's a pot of gold guarded by leprechauns at the end of it.
   - Seeing a double rainbow brings you luck the rest of the day.
   - Touching a rainbow will make you disappear.

   > This is ridiculous. I think she made this last one up. Google it later.

Summary: Rainbows seem commonplace, but it takes a perfect alignment of circumstances and people to actually see one, which explains why people made superstitious myths about them.

## HASH MASH: RAINBOWS

**Definition:
  - An arch of light
  - A curved spectrum of parallel colors shining through falling water droplets either at the end of a rain shower or in a waterfall
  - Appears in early morning or late afternoon

**Colors are:
  - Red—ripe tomato, "stop" light, ruby
  - Orange—tangerine
  - Yellow—ripe banana, butter, "slow" light
  - Green—live pine tree, fresh spinach, "go" light
  - Blue—cloudless sky
  - Indigo—blueberry stains on your white shirt
  - Violet—blackberry stains on your white shirt

**Common myths:
  - There's a pot of gold guarded by leprechauns at the end of it.
  - Seeing a double rainbow brings you luck the rest of the day.
  - Touching a rainbow will make you disappear—I've never heard this before. I think she made it up.

# SPIDER MAPPING: RAINBOWS

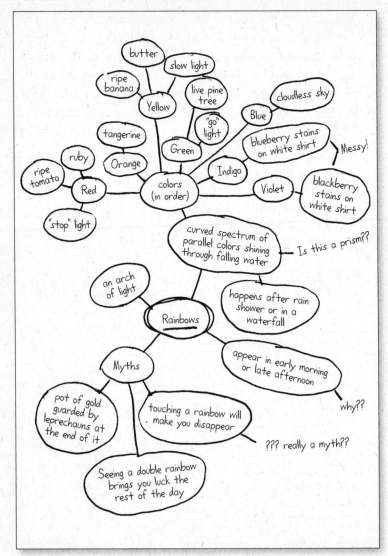

butter
slow light
ripe banana
Yellow
live pine tree
cloudless sky
Blue
"go" light
Green
blueberry stains on white shirt
Messy!
tangerine
Orange
Indigo
Violet
blackberry stains on white shirt
ripe tomato
ruby
Red
colors (in order)
"stop" light
curved spectrum of parallel colors shining through falling water
Is this a prism??
an arch of light
happens after rain shower or in a waterfall
Rainbows
Myths
appear in early morning or late afternoon
pot of gold guarded by leprechauns at the end of it
touching a rainbow will make you disappear
why??
??? really a myth??
Seeing a double rainbow brings you luck the rest of the day

## THE MODEL MODEL: RAINBOWS

If I were to design my own three-dimensional model of notes on rainbows, I'd need some paint, sponges, cardboard, tin foil, and a cheap mini-flashlight. I'd probably also need some clip-art of a leprechaun and a four-leaf clover for the myths section, and I'd have to brainstorm a bit on how to show the last myth about the rainbow making someone disappear. However, that's just what I would use to build a freestanding arch showing the full display of color as created by the prism effect of light cut by water. What would you use?

## THE ENDGAME: RAINBOWS

This Round Two note card includes information from the other notes you would have collected that week, summarizing all five of the teacher's lectures on "light," including the first lecture notes on rainbows.

---

Light, Color, Prisms
Rainbows
— ROY G BIV color spectrum
— after rain or in a waterfall
— angle of reflection from sun, to water drops, to eyesight must be 40-42 degrees
— double rainbow: above the perfect bow is a dimmer bow with colors in reversed order
Prism
— triangular glass
— takes in white light and bends it into mini-rainbow

— has a similar refractive index to waterfalls, creating rainbows
Light
— looks white, but made of full spectrum
— can travel in a vacuum
— consists of electric and magnetic energy called electromagnetic radiation
— has wavelengths and vibrations

---

# Appendix C:
# Time Maps

|  | SUN | MON | TUE | WED | THR | FRI | SAT |
|---|---|---|---|---|---|---|---|
| 7 A.M. | | Swim practice | | Swim practice | | Swim practice | |
| 8 A.M. | | S | S | S | S | S | |
| 9 A.M. | | C | C | C | C | C | |
| 10 A.M. | | H | H | H | H | H | |
| 11 A.M. | | O | O | O | O | O | |
| NOON | | O | O | O | O | O | |
| 1 P.M. | | L | L | L | L | L | |
| 2 P.M. | | ! | ! | ! | ! | ! | |
| 3 P.M. | | Violin lesson | Strength training | Practice violin | Strength training | Practice violin | |
| 4 P.M. | | Study | Practice violin | Study | Practice violin | Study | |
| 5 P.M. | | Study | Study | Study | Study | Study | |
| 6 P.M. | | | | | | | |
| 7 P.M. | | Volunteer @ soup kitchen | | | | | |
| 8 P.M. | | | | | Watch my favorite show | | |

# Appendix D:
# Sample Study Group Schedule

Meeting start time: _____
Meeting end time: _____
Location: _____

1. Points of confusion from last week's lectures and discussions

2. Points of confusion from last week's readings

3. Points of confusion for current homework assignments

4. Brainstorming for upcoming project assignments

5. Study games to help prep for upcoming exams

6. Final comments or questions

7. Snacks!

# Appendix E:
# Learning Disability Resources

**Ann Logsdon—Learning Disabilities Resource Guide at About.com.**
learningdisabilities.about.com

**Child Development Institute (CDI)**
www.childdevelopmentinfo.com

**Council for Learning Disabilities (CLD)**
Phone: 913-491-1011 • www.cldinternational.org

**Education Resources Information Center (ERIC)**
Toll-free Phone: 1-800-LET-ERIC (800-538-3742) • www.eric.ed.gov

**LD OnLine**
www.ldonline.org

**Learning Disabilities Association (LDA) of America**
Phone: (412) 341-1515 • www.ldanatl.org

**National Center for Learning Disabilities (NCLD)**
Phone: (212) 545-7510 • Toll-free Information and Referral Service:
1-888-575-7373 • www.ncld.org

## CANADIAN RESOURCES
**Learning Disabilities Association of Canada (LDAC)**
Toll-free Phone: 1-877-238-5332 • www.ldac-taac.ca

# ACKNOWLEDGMENTS

I've often thought the acknowledgments section should be renamed something like "The White Pages of Gratitude" because a book is made possible only by the help and determination of so many who deserve to be thanked, but their long list of names may read a bit like the phone book. For the sake of all those trees we mentioned earlier, I'll keep it brief. You have studying to do, after all.

I must start at the beginning by thanking my former students at Northern and Jordan High Schools, who were gracious enough to launch me into my teaching career, giving me all sorts of fodder and inspiration to initially develop this material as a handout. Some of you will find your stories here. While you were the inspiration for this book, my students enlisted in the US Army in Seoul, Korea, at Yongsan Garrison, Camp Kim, Camp Coiner, Camp Red Cloud, and Camp Casey, gave me an even greater dedication to the project; I am grateful to you most importantly for your service to our country but also for insisting that my simple study handout was timely and greatly needed, encouraging me to develop it into this book.

If my students were the heart behind the book, my colleagues, agent, and editors were the hands. An immeasurable thank you to Brian Cooper, Jett Parsley, Hollace Selph, and Shayne Goodrum for equipping and encouraging me as a teacher, especially in those early days when my naïve idealism was probably nauseating. A super-huge "Roerig's World" thank you to Todd Roerig for introducing me to Sandra Bullard, and combining your forty years of teaching experience to suggest improvements for this book, making it "cake;" thank you to students Dax Roerig and Erin Bullard for your fresh perspectives on the book as well. I send armfuls of gratitude to Jen Nelson and her freshmen at Overlake High

School, who made chapter three a class project and sent back lots of great feedback. Thanks, also, to Ann Logsdon for your expert feedback on learning disabilities in the final chapter of this book as we neared publication. Thank you to Rita Rosenkranz for your sophisticated professionalism in helping this book meander through a forest of contracts and find its way. I am especially grateful to have Chris Kalb adding his unique artistic wit to this project after admiring his work for many years. A special thank you to my editor, Veronica Randall, for your creativity and skill at capturing the vision for this book and pushing it to the next level, keeping your sense of humor (and mine) intact all the while. And, thanks again to Aaron Wehner, Colleen Cain, Ashley Thompson, freelance copyeditor Leslie Baylor, and the friendly folks at Ten Speed Press and, now, Random House/Crown, who have welcomed me on yet another venture onto the bookshelf.

While all these people helped bring this book to the page, none were as instrumental or deserve greater thanks than my husband, Joshua. It seems like all authors thank their spouses in some way, but truly I would not have had the endurance to develop and publish this book were it not for the tireless support and freedom you have given me to pursue my best work. You have made me the happiest of women.

And finally, thanks to you, dear reader, for allowing me into your world and inviting me on your scholastic journey. May your work fill you with great satisafaction and may all your hard efforts lead to doors swinging wide with opportunity.

# INDEX

# ABOUT THE AUTHOR

Author, poet, and educator **ANNE CROSSMAN** made her publishing debut as coauthor, with Peter Feaver and Sue Wasiolek, of *Getting the Best Out of College: A Professor, a Dean, and a Student Tell You How to Maximize Your Experience* (Ten Speed Press, 2008).

After studying at Stanford and Duke Universities, earning a BA in English and a Certificate of Education, Anne began a career in education by teaching in public high schools, military barracks, and around kitchen tables to students ranging from academic underdogs to honor society prodigies. It was this experience coupled with her desire to see students aim for and achieve their best which largely inspired this book

Anne's work has been published in notable sources such as the *Washington Post, Margie,* and *Nimrod,* and she has recently published her first book of poems, *Trying to Remember,* a memoir about Alzheimer's. She is a recovering Unperfected Perfectionist.

Visit www.AnneCrossman.com.